ONCE UPON A RHYME

IMAGINATION FOR A NEW GENERATION

Co Durham
Edited by Steve Twelvetree

 Young**Writers**

First published in Great Britain in 2004 by:
Young Writers
Remus House
Coltsfoot Drive
Peterborough
PE2 9JX
Telephone: 01733 890066
Website: www.youngwriters.co.uk

SB ISBN 1 84400 430 0

Foreword

Young Writers was established in 1991 and has been passionately devoted to the promotion of reading and writing in children and young adults ever since. The quest continues today. Young Writers remains as committed to engendering the fostering of burgeoning poetic and literary talent as ever.

This year's Young Writers competition has proven as vibrant and dynamic as ever and we are delighted to present a showcase of the best poetry from across the UK. Each poem has been carefully selected from a wealth of *Once Upon A Rhyme* entries before ultimately being published in this, our twelfth primary school poetry series.

Once again, we have been supremely impressed by the overall high quality of the entries we have received. The imagination, energy and creativity which has gone into each young writer's entry made choosing the best poems a challenging and often difficult but ultimately hugely rewarding task - the general high standard of the work submitted amply vindicating this opportunity to bring their poetry to a larger appreciative audience.

We sincerely hope you are pleased with our final selection and that you will enjoy *Once Upon A Rhyme Co Durham* for many years to come.

Contents

Kate Thompson (10)	26
Euan Torano (10)	26
Helen Court (10)	27
Adam Cooper (11)	27
Michael Brunell (11)	28
Adam Dale (10)	28
Daniel Alderson (9)	29
Bradley Layton (9)	29
Kelsey Maughan (9)	30
Josh Harper (9)	30
Mary Moore (10)	31
James Thwaites (9)	32
Philip Merryweather (9)	32
Jordan Thompson Parkin (10)	33
Joseph Brown (10)	33
Alice Wood (9)	34
Stacey Walker (7)	34
Robert Mounter (8)	34
Rebecca Watson (9)	35
Fiona Cook (9)	35
Kieran Briggs (8)	36
Emily Bonnett (9)	36
Craig Torano (8)	36
Amy Tones (8)	37
Isobel Thomas (8)	37
Rory Lincoln (7)	37
Lauren Smith (9)	38
Edward Harding (8)	38
Bryony Gargett (8)	38
Lucy Scott (9)	39
Jessica Moore (7)	39
Amy Lowson (7)	39
Natalie Hobson (9)	40
Jennifer Healy (8)	40
Shannon Toole (10)	41
Samantha Berry (9)	41
Jake Gargett (10)	42
Jack Holguin (8)	42
Charlotte Dye (9)	43
Ian Bell (9)	43
Alice Carr (9)	44
Sarah Hanson (10)	45

Robert Dixon (9)   45
Danielle Cassidy (9)   46
Jonathan Foster (9)   46
Ben Ball (11)   47
Adam Black (10)   47
Jamie Holder (11)   48
Harley Oliver (7)   48
Elisabeth Harding (10)   49
Matthew Bainbridge (10)   49
Matthew Brough (11)   50
Andrew Scott (11)   50
Paige Wilkinson (9)   51
Sarah Teasdale (8)   51
Liam Brown (9)   52
Natalie Garner (7)   52

Dodmire Junior School
Rachel Tunstall (10)   53
Philip Stephenson (10)   53
Jordan Green (9)   53
Natasha Bennett (9)   54
David Freak (10)   54
Thomas Taylor (10)   54
Abbie Luck (9)   55
Luke Swannell (9)   55
Nicholas Wiper (9)   56
Caramon Collinson (9)   56
Olivia Johnson (10)   57
Conor Davies (10)   57
Jessica Elve (10)   58
Corey Aldus (9)   58
Annastasia Wade (9)   58
Susan Sung (11)   59
Rebecca-Naomi Littlefair (11)   59
Natalie Winter (11)   60
Benjamin Snowball (9)   60
Robert Ward (10)   61
Susan Glew (11)   61
Tegan Stevenson (9)   62
Georgina Wade (9)   63
Jack Littlefair (8)   63

Alanna Stevenson (7)	63
Stephen Richardson (10)	64
Kathryn Woolston (11)	64
Nathaniel Wilson (8)	64
Jason Watt (7)	65
Hayley Jemmett (10)	65
Tallia Cornforth (10)	65
Sophie Pursey (8)	66
Andrew Pitt (10)	66
Chelsea McIntyre (8)	67
Liam Greaves (9)	67
Heather Smith-Burns (8)	67
Jack Tenwick (9)	68
Laura Nickson (9)	68
Lewis McIntyre (10)	69
Louise Chapman (9)	69
Andrew Elliott (10)	70
George Ward (10)	70
James Cooke (10)	70
Richard Sung (10)	71
Sarah Bamber (9)	71
Jonathan Robinson (10)	71
Anthony Watt (10)	72
Graeme Briggs (10)	72
Michaela Mullett (8)	73
Amy Sung (9)	73
Thomas Heath (9)	74
Victoria Monk (7)	74
David Lonsdale (11)	75
Jordan Connelly (11)	75
Joshua Ward (8)	76
Aarun Toor (11)	76
Rachel Chapman (8)	77
Mitchell Woodward (8)	77
Ashley Ruddam (9)	77
Rosie Elve (9)	78
Charlotte Roscoe (8)	78
Andrew Robinson (8)	79
Sarah Thompson (11)	80
Thomas Roscoe (8)	81
John Wilson (8)	81
Daisy Arrowsmith (8)	82

Melissa Holmes (8)	82
Maria Jane Smith (8)	83
Lewis Myers (9)	83
Daniel Toth (8)	84
Emma McAfee (10)	84
Jack Carson (9)	85
Lucy Earnshaw (9)	85
Rachael Sturdy (9)	85

Hartside Primary School

Arrianne Nelson (9)	86
Rebecca Winter (9)	86
Kurt Readman (9)	87
Adrian Adamson (9)	87
Laura George (10)	87
Stacey Parkinson (8)	88
Megan Bryden (7)	88
Lauren Moore (8)	89
Connor Thompson (8)	89
Megan Scott (8)	90
Rebecca Pinder (8)	90
Katie Leigh (8)	90
Dominic Woloszyn (8)	91
Jamie-Lee Harding (9)	91
Rachel Sewell (8)	91
Emma Winter (9)	92
Beth Moralee (9)	92
Stefan Johnson (8)	93
Kaylee Pollitt (9)	93
Claire Hodkinson (10)	94
Ellie Burns (8)	94
Bethany Howcroft (8)	94
Hannah Blakey (7)	95
Natalie Hopper (8)	95
Scott Lavery (7)	95
Evan Conley (7)	96
Ethan Campbell (8)	96
Samantha Sleights (8)	96
Kalan Roberts (7)	97
Jacob Craig (7)	97
Holly Howe (8)	97

Meghan Nicholson (7)	98
Daniel Lawson (8)	98
Georgina Parker (7)	98
Thomas Mason (10)	99
Holly Dixon (10)	99
Ryan Scott (8)	99
Anthony Gale (9)	100
Holly Craig (10)	100
Callum Futter (9)	100
Shelby Timoney (9)	101
Lauren Hutchinson (10)	101
Beth Dawson (9)	101
Matthew Allan (10)	102
Kayleigh Abbott (10)	102
Stephanie Parker (9)	102
Alex Hall (10)	103

Hunwick Primary School

Anya Campbell (9)	103
Lucy Hedley (8)	103
Jasmine Graham (8)	104
Wallis Greaves (8)	104
Rebecca Hawthorne (9)	104
Josh Keig (9)	105
Daniel Bennett (8)	105
Stephanie Bennett (8)	105
Biancha Tarran (10)	106
Laura Bradshaw (8)	106
Callum Hodgson (9)	106
Sally Pentecost (8)	107
Lauren Hawthorne (9)	107
Nicole Green (9)	108
Megan Maddison (8)	108
Chloe Green (9)	109
Jamie Campbell (9)	109
Alex Bradshaw (8)	110
Ellie Pryce (9)	110

Ingleton CE Primary School

Freddie Metcalfe (9)	110
Jon Ainsley (11)	111

Bethany Payne (9)   111
Hilly Redgrave (11)   112
Annabel Franks (9)   112
Sam Hunter (9)   112
Kayleigh Toms (10)   113
Daniel Westgarth (10)   113
Alexander Clark (10)   113
Samuel Forster (10)   113
Oliver Armstrong (9)   114
Charlotte Marshall (11)   114
Peter K Armstrong (10)   114
Adam Bourne (10)   115
Rebecca Parker (10)   115
Samantha Weatherburn (11)   115

Mowden Junior School

Emma Sisk (9)   116
Nicola Dennis (10)   117
Connie Archer (7)   117
Ian Wilson (9)   118
Sarah Grainger (10)   118
Jennifer English (8)   119
Jessica Burton (9)   120
Stephanie Wilson (7)   120
Danielle Murdock (8)   121
Sam Shield (8)   121
Connor Shield (8)   122
Lauren McQuaker (11)   122
Calum Williams (10)   123
Isabel Walker (7)   123
Matthew Hewitson (10)   124
Liam Innis (9)   124
Joshua Egglestone (10)   125
Jonathan Morgan (10)   125
Shaun Bradley (10)   126
Jordan Lauder (11)   126
Michael Hahn (10)   127
David Wilson (11)   128
Liam Lynch (8)   128
Matthew Rowan (10)   129
Leanne Jones (11)   129

Brooklyn Armstrong (9)	130
Zohrah Malik (9)	131
Nicholas Gordon (11)	132
Iona Hill (10)	133
Emily Kent (10)	134
Gregory Boulby (11)	134
Jonathan Coates (9)	135
David Freary (10)	135
Adam Craig (10)	136
Robert Smith (9)	137
Beth Tulloch (8)	138
Ryan Blewitt (10)	138
Catherine Parnaby (9)	139
James Philip (10)	139
David Woodward (10)	139
Nicole Pinder (10)	140
Emma Bartram (10)	140
Jared Kelvey-Brown (11)	141
Nicholas Bruce (11)	141
Matthew Gosling (10)	142
William Whittaker (9)	142
Marran Turner (9)	143
Harriet Walker (10)	144
Christopher Dove (11)	144
Stephanie Coates (10)	145
Lily Thompson (9)	145
Jonathan Wilkes (11)	146
Jade Edwardson (8)	146
Niamh Caverhill (8)	147
Nathan Braithwaite (10)	147
Frances Hodgson (9)	148
Jade McGarrell (9)	148
Hannah Smith (11)	149
Taylor Weeks (9)	149
Andrew Barnes (10)	150
Lauren Turner (9)	150
James Dobson (10)	151
Declan Gegg (10)	151
Rebecca Wilson (9)	152
Alice Morley (8)	152
Hannah Ferguson (10)	153
Kieran Lynch (9)	154

Emily Ingleson (10)	154
Kerry Holliday (10)	155
Caitlin Stalker (9)	155
Samantha Corner (10)	156
Grace Edwards (10)	156
Jack Whittaker (10)	157
Keziah Morley (10)	157
Louise Bracken (8)	158
Hannah Dennis (8)	158
Charlotte Foster (9)	159
Lucy O'Neill (9)	160
Andrew Page (10)	161
Kathryn Binks (9)	161
Becky Mutton (9)	162
Rebecca Bynoe (9)	163
Yasmin Peckitt-Singh (8)	164
Jenny Stalker (11)	165
Shaun Gault (11)	166

Ouston Junior School

Christopher Wiseman (10)	166
Rachel Laidler (10)	167
Kay Pearson (11)	167
Kyle Wilson (9)	168
Daniel Empson (10)	168
Amy Marsden (9)	168
Bethany Findlay (10)	169
Lauren Andrews (9)	169
Andrew Mollett (10)	169
Katrina Small (11)	170
Lilyanna Turner (9)	170
Adam Kirkup (10)	170
Brogan Stephenson (10)	171
Mikki Clark (9)	171
Adam Rowe (8)	171
Harpreet Singh Jhally (10)	172
Shonagh Glass (10)	172
Ryan Edgar (10)	172
Liam Twomey (8)	173
Abbie Carr (9)	173
Gemma Heron (9)	174

Kate Driver (9)	174
Ben Holden (9)	175
Daniel Hawthorne (8)	175
Sophie Taylor (9)	176
Amy Kingston (8)	176
Charlotte Hogg (9)	177
Katie Hampson (10)	177
Lois Bridgewood (11)	178
Alexander Rowe (10)	178
Samantha Bright (9)	179
Nathan Cooper (10)	179
Dean Smith (9)	179
Sarah Currie (9)	180
Christopher Hunter (9)	180
Andrew Spurr (9)	180
Rachel Cockburn (10)	181
Katie McGuire (9)	181
Bethany Cockburn (9)	181
Jessica Morrow (10)	182
Bradley Gray (10)	182
Sophie Patterson (9)	182
Samantha Brown (11)	183
Olivia Douglass (8)	183
Adam Hunt (10)	184
Emma Luker (9)	184
Helen Briggs (10)	185
Stephen Mollett (10)	185
Rachael Yeadon (10)	186
Jack Thirlwell (10)	186
Simon Tyrrell (10)	186
Daniel Nicholson (9)	187
Rachael Miley (9)	187
Phillip Pearson (9)	187
Kris Bambynek (10)	188
Alex Moody (10)	188
Laura Kerry (10)	188
Laura McDermott (10)	189
Samuel Johnson (10)	189
Jonathan Forster (10)	189
Robyn Clark (9)	190
Andrew Ellison (9)	190
Danielle Gleadhill (9)	190

Anna Drake (9)	191
Matthew Laybourn (10)	191
Richard Young (9)	191
Olivia Bradbury (8)	192
Jennifer Waite (8)	192
Jessica Guy (8)	192
Amy Murray (9)	193
Philip Brown (9)	193
Emmy Brown (10)	194
Jessica Anderson (9)	194
Charlotte Slaymaker (9)	194

Raventhorpe Preparatory School

Ram Prasana Jambulingam (10)	195
Debbie Cheesbrough (11)	195
Adam Matthews (10)	196
Victoria Richardson (10)	197
Cheryl Gartland (11)	197
Harriet Peacock (11)	198
Alexandra Thompson (9)	198
Victoria Whitaker (10)	199
Hannah Hillary (11)	199
Danielle Overfield (10)	200
Oliver Whitchurch (9)	200
James Mitchinson (10)	201
Peter Stephens (9)	201
Simon Warne (9)	202
Nicole Burlinson (10)	203
Charlotte Alderson (10)	203
Saif Khalil (9)	204
Andrew Nicholson (9)	204

Sunnybrow Primary School

Anthony Pardew (9)	204
Chloe Thompson (10)	205
Ross Stoker (10)	206
Anthony Kirsopp (9)	206
Laura Bartlett (10)	207
Thomas Garrod (10)	207
Chloe Woolf (10)	208
Craig Allinson (11)	208

Ryan Liddell (9)   209
Connor Coulson (11)   209
Luke Newton (9)   210
Shannen Wilson (9)   210
Rachael Thompson (9)   210
James Matthews (8)   211
Chelsea Stoker (9)   211

The Chorister School
Rory Adey (9)   211
Jacob Bushnell (7)   212
Aidan Jagger (9)   212
Charlotte Tait (8)   212
Piers Broadfoot (11)   213
Alice Brown (9)   213
Oisín Keating (9)   214
Elliot Macdonald (9)   214
Samuel Storer (10)   215
Elliot Lydon (9)   215
Alice Doherty (11)   216
Holly Lindley (9)   216
Georgia Forbes (10)   217
Alex Goulding (8)   217
John-Paul Moberly (9)   218
John Anderson (10)   218
Thomas Lydon (10)   219
Henry Pemberton (11)   219
James Matthews (10)   220
William Dooley (10)   220
Freddie Wintrip (11)   221
Adam Waugh (9)   221
Lyndsay Connor (9)   222
Sophie Phillips (11)   223
Dominic Cockburn (10)   223
James Roberts (10)   224

The Poems

My Magic Box

(Based on 'Magic Box' by Kit Wright)

My magic box is made from the freshness of fox's skin from
the countryside.

My magic box is the shape of a glistening golden stone from
my grandad's mine.

My magic box opens with the sound of Bruce Springsteen singing
'War' in front of millions of people.

I will keep in my magic box the sight of the first sound wave rushing
to my ear.
I will keep in my magic box the sight of light rushing to my eyes.
I will keep in my magic box the sound of a newborn dog crying.
I will keep in my magic box the sound of the last school bell when
many children become excited.

I will keep in my magic box the taste of fine foods which
nobody can afford.
I will keep in my magic box the smell of the fresh country air.
I will keep in my magic box the fresh baked pies on a
hot summer's day.

I will keep in my magic box the feel of England winning
the World Cup.
I will keep in my magic box the feel of winning the lottery.

My magic box will close with a cry from a young boy who
despises war.

In my magic box I will keep the dream of living in Candyland
where I will gobble toffee and chocs forever.

John Lumsdon (10)
Barnard Castle CE Primary School

Mia's Magic Box

(Based on 'Magic Box' by Kit Wright)

My magic box is fashioned with the sweet scent of a ruby-red rose.
My magic box is shaped like a glistening giant sunset and a soothing
touch of an angel.
My magic box opens with a silky touch from a scaly slithering snake
and a calm smile of a jet-black dragon.
I will keep in my box the glistening glow of a shiny shooting star and
the first flash of thunder and lightning.
I will keep in my box a sweet, gentle guardian angel sitting
in an everlasting wishing well and the gorgeous smell of
freshly baked biscuits.
I will keep in my box a flame from a flame-thrower and a secret
no one knows.
I will keep in my box a flickering spark of a firework and a big hug
from my mum.
I will keep in my box the rubbery feeling of a squeaky dolphin and a
luxury Lamborghini.
My magic box closes with the graceful moves of a buzzing bumblebee
and a tickle from a heavenly fluttering feather.
I and my magic box will travel all round the wondrous world.

Mia Seymour (10)
Barnard Castle CE Primary School

Love And Hate

The thing I love about my rabbit is its fluffy fur,
The thing I hate about my dog is its breath,
The thing I love about my mother is her cuddles,
The thing I hate about my room is it's always messy,
The thing I love about my bike is its stunts,
The thing I hate about my bike is I always fall off,
The thing I love about my friends is their friendship,
The thing I hate about my skateboard is it's broken,
The thing I love about my weekends is I get to do anything,
The thing I hate about my dad is I never get to see him,
The thing I love about my dad is he never forgets my birthday,
The thing I hate about my electric scooter is the charging.

Marcus Jackson (10)
Barnard Castle CE Primary School

Ruth's Magic Box

(Based on 'Magic Box' by Kit Wright)

My magic box is fashioned with a graceful, glistening, glamorous dose
of never-ending love which sings sweetly as you observe
the lace lid.
My magic box is the shape of a ruby-red, silk love heart,
with a glistening diamond chandelier engraved in the middle.
My magic box opens with a triumphant twitch from a unicorn,
with a smooth firm horn stylishly formed on its furry forelock.
In my magic box I will keep a gentle kiss from my mum,
a praise from my compassionate teacher and a spike from
a hedgehog.
In my magic box I will keep a note from my favourite song,
a wand from a flowery fairy and an ember from a dying fire.
In my magic box I will keep the last smile from my uncle,
a wing from a holy angel and a loving hug from my gran.
In my magic box I will keep a dive from a dappled dolphin,
a laugh from my dad and a tear from a friend.
My magic box will close with a flutter from a flying arrow from Cupid.
In my box I will travel to the snowy surface of Utah,
where I can glide down the pure white mountains.

Ruth Bracegirdle (11)
Barnard Castle CE Primary School

My Magic Box!

(Based on 'Magic Box' by Kit Wright)

My magic box is made from clear water from the turquoise sea and
the distant shimmer from a diamond.
My magic box is the shape of nothingness, it is something
no one can see.
My magic box opens with the giggles of my best friend and the
silent twinkle of a star.
In my magic box I will keep an unfinished dream, a purr from my cat,
a future I haven't seen yet, a thought of my family, a kiss from my mum
and an uncaught thought.
My magic box will close with the peaceful sound of silence.
My magic box will make sure everyone is safe.

Jessica Thomas (11)
Barnard Castle CE Primary School

Lauren's Magic Box

(Based on 'Magic Box' by Kit Wright)

My magic box is made from the embrace of a glamorous, magical
fairy with cushioned satin wings.
My magic box is a sculpture of a butterfly's delicate dazzling wings
and as petite as a fairy's precious foot.
My magic box opens with the development of a brand new rosebud
and a wail from a newborn baby.

In my magic box I will keep the touch of a fish's smooth,
scaly substance,
the sight of air everlasting ice cream melting,
the smell of a rose's unforgettable scent,
the thud of Big Ben's deafening clock ticking,
the taste of the air in the Sahara desert,
the rarest diamond in the world,
the biggest gobstopper the world has ever seen,
a memory of a supreme spaghetti Bolognese,
the first snowflake ever floundered.

My magic box closes with the rise of the buttercup sun on an icy day.
In my magic box I will perch inside a gleaming bubble, floating in
a warm, cuddly bath.

Lauren Thwaites (11)
Barnard Castle CE Primary School

Things I Have Loved

These I have loved;
The hot sun blazing over the green, green grass,
Beautiful red roses growing behind yellow tulips,
White snowdrops rising after the dark dull winter,
The look of the sea-blue rivers that whirl around in the summer,
The smell of the yellow beaches glowing like gold in
                                    the gloomy moonlight,
The taste of autumn under the wintry showers,
Restaurants full of lovely candlelight.

Jodie Proffitt (9)
Barnard Castle CE Primary School

Jemma-May's Magic Box

(Based on 'Magic Box' by Kit Wright)

My magic box is made of a silk teddy bear you can cuddle into with
pearl eyes and angel's wings as paws.
My magic box is the shape of a gigantic teddy bear, the size of
a skyscraper with the shine of a crystal against the sun.
My magic box opens with a sprinkle of fairy dust and the turn of a
glittering ruby-red key and the roar of the magical sea against the
large brown coloured rocks.
In my box I will keep the warmest cuddle from my mum,
the happiest memories of the past,
the diamonds of the sky-lit rainbow,
the sand of a flutter from an enormous eagle's wing,
the flickering flame of a fire burning daringly,
the sound of a freely flowing waterfall.

My magic box closes slowly and sneakily with the turn of a glittering
glitterball and the sound of children singing to disco songs.
My magic box is the colours of the pearl-like ocean and the
diamonds that lay on the seabed.
In my box I will visit all of my relatives around the world and share
all my magical, marvellous millions with my friends.

Jemma-May Knight (10)
Barnard Castle CE Primary School

These I Have Loved

The sparkling sun shimmering over the palm trees
In the hot summer's sky,
Cold snow getting thrown at me
And making beautiful crystal clear snowmen,
Restaurants, the lovely music playing away in the far meadows,
Rugby, when I was chosen to be in the Tag Rugby Festival,
Lollies, the gentle coldness in your tender mouth,
Poppies, the smell, it's like strawberries dipped in sugar,
Football, it's like people to watch and people to play in teams
And to give them skills in their feet.

Adam Smith (9)
Barnard Castle CE Primary School

Simon's Magic Box

(Based on 'Magic Box' by Kit Wright)

My magic box is made from sparkling diamond-green
Snakeskin and razor-sharp crocodile teeth.

My magic box is shaped like a fierce gliding eagle
With a beak that is so strong it could knock down a house.

My box opens with a great explosion from a dangerous volcano.

In my magic box I will keep the huge roar of a mad crowd
When Jeff Hurst scored for England in the World Cup.

The magical shot of a bow,
A flash of powerful red-hot lightning as it chops down a tree,
A shooting star as I make a wish.

My magic box closes at the sound of a dangerous stampede
From an elephant herd and a colourful firework
When it goes high in the sky.

Simon Fawcett (11)
Barnard Castle CE Primary School

Daniel's Magic Box

(Based on 'Magic Box' by Kit Wright)

My magic box is made from lizard skin
And teeth from a dinosaur,
With legs from a cheetah.
My magic box is shaped like a flying falcon,
With rough wings and a monster smile.
My magic box opens with the sound from ACDC in concert.
In my magic box I will keep a golden sword
And the reddest ruby and the fastest dragon bite.
I will also keep a magic wish from a shooting star
And the magical magic dust.
My magic box will take me to the best motocross track in the world.
My magic box closes with the roar from a tormented tiger.
My magic box is the best ever.

Daniel Rudge (11)
Barnard Castle CE Primary School

Sophie's Magic Box

(Based on 'Magic Box' by Kit Wright)

My magic box is made from a glistening shiny red rose
with silky soft petals.

My magic box is the shape of a shiny silky smooth
goldfish's tail.

My magic box opens with a touch of a naughty pussy
cat's mischievous whiskers.

In my magic box I will keep a soft puppy-dog's tail.
In my magic box I will keep the sparkles and sunshine of
a glittering star.
In my magic box I will keep happy memories.
In my magic box I will keep my dead fish, Fred.

In my magic box I will keep the touch of an angel's hand.
In my magic box I will keep the scent of lavender soft.
In my magic box I will keep all of my secrets.
In my magic box I will keep the kiss of my mum.

In my magic box I will keep the snore of my brother.
In my magic box I will keep a secret supply of chocolate.
In my magic box I will keep my favourite teddies.
In my magic box I will keep the smell of Sunday dinner.

My box will travel to Cyprus in the warm sun.

Sophie Foster (10)
Barnard Castle CE Primary School

Tiger

The tiger has a furry orange coat,
With black lightning spears sewn on.
As the biggest cat, it is deadly in water as on land,
Its coat helps it to camouflage its large body.
It seeks its prey, keeps low and strikes,
Back at its den, it sleeps with a full belly
With a carcass in front of it,
It doesn't wake until another day.

Shona Dixen (10)
Barnard Castle CE Primary School

My Magic Box

(Based on 'Magic Box' by Kit Wright)

My magic box is made from the smell of a ruby-red tulip,
With soft, silky petals and a glistening stem.
My magic box is the shape of a glittering golden star,
Filled with precious diamonds.
My magic box opens by the thought of a fairy's kiss
And the sound of her fluttering wings.
In my magic box I will keep . . .
The thought of the clouds in Heaven,
A taste from a chocolate heart,
A piece from the sun in the brightest sky,
A touch from an angel's wing,
The touch from a shooting star,
A burn from a fearsome fire,
The first tear from a baby,
A purr from my cat.
My magic box closes by the sound of an angel's harp.
My magic box will take me to a land of eternal chocolate.

Zoe Raine (10)
Barnard Castle CE Primary School

My Magic Box

(Based on 'Magic Box' by Kit Wright)

My magic box is made of the taste of a creamy chocolate éclair
that has been freshly made.
My magic box is the shape of a luscious heart
surrounded with sharp daring spikes.
My magic box opens with the cold touch of a fairy's kiss.
In my box I will keep a warm hug from my mum.
In my box I will keep the memory of my holiday in Turkey.
In my box I will keep an everlasting supply of wishes.
In my box I will keep one thousand secrets.
In my box I will keep the only picture of my lost grandad.
In my box I will keep the feeling of Christmas morning.
My box will close with the sound of snowbells ringing.
In my box I will dance with Justin Timberlake.

Chantelle Weatherill (11)
Barnard Castle CE Primary School

My Magic Box

(Based on 'Magic Box' by Kit Wright)

My magic box is made of a glistening golden gate to Heaven,
with a calming smell of a new morning.

My magic box is the shape of a ruby-red key of wisdom,
with a handle the shape of a lion's sneaky face.

My magic box opens with the moo of a newborn calf,
taking its first steps on fresh golden straw.

In my magic box I will keep a pixie with pointed ears
giggling amusingly at the circus,
a huge pile of diamonds daringly found at the bottom of the ocean,
the feeling of winning the rugby World Cup for England,
a memory of my late dog, Simba with the heart of a lion,
a jar of freshly baked chocolate chip biscuits,
an amount of money I could only dream of,
the extinct T-rex,
my guardian angel watching over my family and wherever we go,
the everlasting heart that will let me live forever,
as many wishes as I could wish for,
the will to do anything and a hug from all my family.

My magic box will close with the flip of a blue whale's tail
In the turquoise sea underneath the rising buttercup sun.

My magic box will take me to the Olympic Games
where I shall triumph in every race.

Emma Coupland (11)
Barnard Castle CE Primary School

My Magic Box

(Based on 'Magic Box' by Kit Wright)

My brilliant magic box is made of the finest gold imagined by man.
My brilliant magic box is shaped like a waterfall splashing
into the river.
My brilliant magic box opens with a knock and the tune of the
National Anthem.
In my brilliant magic box I will keep the feeling of scoring the third
goal in a hat-trick.
In my brilliant magic box I will keep the moment England lifted
the World Cup.
In my brilliant magic box I will keep the first time that I
kicked a football.
In my brilliant magic box I will keep the first time that I swam
without armbands.
In my brilliant magic box I will keep the adrenalin rush I got when
I first rode a roller coaster.
In my brilliant magic box I will keep the moment my brother was born.
In my brilliant magic box I will keep the first time that I smelt the sea.
In my brilliant magic box I will keep the first football match I ever saw.
In my brilliant magic box I will keep my dead dog, Ben's spirit.
In my brilliant magic box I will keep the first born lamb in spring.
In my brilliant magic box I will keep a robin's song.
In my brilliant magic box I will keep my first ever word.
In my brilliant magic box I will keep a last minute goal by Darlington
to beat Hartlepool in the local derby.
My brilliant magic box will take me to the World Cup final in Brazil
where I will score a hat-trick to win the World Cup for England.
My brilliant magic box only closes when I first play for Darlington.

Richard Stanwix (11)
Barnard Castle CE Primary School

My Magic Box

(Based on 'Magic Box' by Kit Wright)

My magic box is made from everlasting gold chocolate,
Held together with rainbow-flavoured bubblegum
And silver hinges of magic.

My magic box is the shape of a beautiful dream,
Gracefully changing with silver silk lining, smartly winding
Around like a poisonous python.

My box opens with a wicked devilish laugh,
Sneaking in secrets and cruelly hiding them in corners.

In my magic box I will keep . . .
The swish of a dress too expensive for royalty,
The glint of colour from a daring rainbow trout
And the shimmer of sunset on a crystal blue river.

In my magic box I will keep . . .
The feeling of winning the ten million pound lottery,
An alien from an undiscovered planet
And a secret no one knows.

I will also keep in my box . . .
A ferocious tiger to guard me at night,
The whisper of trees
And a never-ending supply of shooting stars to wish upon.

I will also keep in my box . . .
The universe so I can change anything,
An amusing monkey for when I'm sad
And the joy of the first day of the holidays.

In my box I will keep . . .
The smell of Christmas dinner (especially Yorkshire pudding!)
A dinosaur's tooth which millions of years ago chewed
And a man-eating plant that just avoids me.

My box will close with the flutter of fairies,
So small they could compare to brightly coloured beetles.

My box will help me predict the future,
So I will save the world from being destroyed!

Rachel Metcalf (11)
Barnard Castle CE Primary School

My Magic Box
(Based on 'Magic Box' by Kit Wright)

My magic box is made from a rearing, scarlet, shimmering stallion with
eyes like glistening diamonds.

My magic box is the shape of a tempting teddy,
With encrusted emeralds for eyes
And cotton wool for fur that dances in the summer breeze.

My splendid box opens with an enchanted kiss that soars freely
From Heaven and lands upon precious people.

In my magnificent box I will keep a secret whinny from my beloved
Pony in the silent, crisp winter months,
I will also keep a sacred crystal that nobody owns,
That gleams on a stormy moonlit night.

In my magic box I will keep the loving memories of my uncle,
Now he floats with the gentle angels and glittering stars.
In my box I will also keep the sunrise and sunset from Spain,
That jumps from window to window and wavers on the
Royal-blue sea.
In my magic box I will also keep the delicate and divine
Taste of delectable chocolate.

In my delicate box I will keep the thrill of winning one million on TV And
the memory of when I got my pony, I ran around in ecstasy.
I will also keep the joyful sound of my family singing happily together.
In my divine box I will keep the delightful taste of soft sponge
As it melts slowly.
My box will also hold the sound of angels rejoicing.

My magic box closes with a wink of a silver swan swimming
Slowly by with wings like delicate glass.

In my box I will keep the dream of dancing with marshmallow men
On soft fluffy clouds in the sunset where I will play happily
And when the moon shines I will indulge in chocolate.

Rachael Alderson (11)
Barnard Castle CE Primary School

Magic Box

(Based on 'Magic Box' by Kit Wright)

My magic box is made out of blood-red roses with silk petals
and the stalk is made out of the golden sun shining bright.

My magic box is shaped like a big, blue, salty tea
and a green, slippery frog's jump.

My magic box opens with a touch from a magical miniature fairy
and a reflection from a pond.

In my magic box I will keep the loudest roar from a furry friendly tiger.
In my magic box I will keep the feeling of the cool breeze on my face.
In my magic box I will keep the smell of the sparkling,
shimmering, sunlit sea.
In my box I will keep the taste of the richest chocolate ever.

In my box I will keep the rarest stone.
In my box I will keep my friends' giggles.
In my box I will keep everlasting wishes.
In my box I will keep all my precious memories.

My box will close with a click of my fingers and a chirp of a chick
and look down on people and fly anywhere I desire.

Charlotte Slater (11)
Barnard Castle CE Primary School

Magic Box

(Based on 'Magic Box' by Kit Wright)

My box is made of sharp cut diamonds and a python's
poisonous tongue.
My box is shaped like a dead person's coffin.
My box opens with a high-pitched cackle and the tap of my fingers,
In my box I will keep magic dust, a wand and a spying eye.

My box is made of crimson rubies and a dragon's tail.
My box is shaped like a magical castle in a faraway land.
My box opens with a strike of lightning and my ice-cold breath.
In my box I will keep all types of mischievous magical potions.
My box closes with the sound of an angelic angel.

Rachel Wood (11)
Barnard Castle CE Primary School

My Magic Box

(Based on 'Magic Box' by Kit Wright)

My magic box is made of breathtaking fire-blowing
dragon's breath with a vigorous smile.
My magic box is shaped like a hippopotamus' sharp strong horn.
My magic box will open with fierce fighting lions
protecting their young.
In my box I will keep the only ocean star.
In my box I will keep the love of my family.
In my box I will keep the rarest red ruby.
In my box I will keep the world's supply of wishes.
In my box I will keep the shooting star where I placed my wish.

In my box I will keep the laughter of my friends.
In my box I will keep the smallest unicorn.
In my box I will keep the only flying horse.
In my box I will keep the world's biggest diamond.
In my box I will keep the joy when I opened all my presents
on Christmas Day.
In my box I will keep the warmest cuddle from my mum.

In my box I will keep all the money I ever need.
In my box I will keep the surprise of when I got a puppy
for my birthday.
My box will close with the sunshine shooting across the horizon.

In my box I will see my Nanna Bollder and my Grandad
Smithson again.

Rebecca Jackson (11)
Barnard Castle CE Primary School

My Magic Box

(Based on 'Magic Box' by Kit Wright)

My magic box is made from cold hard stone
Dug from the highest hilltop.
My magic box is the shape of a cylindrical stick of dynamite
Glowing in the darkness of the deepest mine.
My magic box opens with the roar of a jet engine
As a plane soars into the sky.
In my magic box I will keep the first time I saw the sea,
A tiger's roar, a robin's song,
The smell of freshly-cut grass, the taste of chocolate,
The joy of school ending, the warmth of a fire,
The sound of Elvis' singing, the thrill of a roller coaster,
The smell of sizzling bacon and a dog's bark,
The memory of blowing out the candles on my birthday cake,
My magic box closes with the end of an era and the closing of an eye,
In my box I will dream of fun times and daring adventures.

Joe Tomlinson (11)
Barnard Castle CE Primary School

Magic Box

(Based on 'Magic Box' by Kit Wright)

My magic box is made of golden sunshine
Which shines like a shooting star.
My magic box is shaped like a colourful butterfly's wings
When it flies into the air as the wind causes danger.
My magic box opens with a powerful speaking voice.

In my box I will keep a magical supply of everlasting money
And precious wishes.
My magic box closes with sparkly, silvery, sharp crocodile teeth,
With a mouth as big as a crispy cookie.

In my magic box I will travel into Heaven,
Where the angels are singing sweetly and softly
In the fluffy clouds.

Frances Pickworth (10)
Barnard Castle CE Primary School

My Magic Box
(Based on 'Magic Box' by Kit Wright)

My magic box is made from a soft, fluffy, cute puppy's fur,
Which is cosy and cuddly.

My magic box is the shape of a glistening kiss from a beautiful
Peaceful angel with cotton wool wings and red ruby hair.

My magic box opens with a twinkle of a glistening star
And the shine of the midnight moon.

In my box I will keep the howl of a wolf in the moonlight
And the bleat of a newborn lamb.

In my box I will keep the taste of a double chocolate chip ice cream
On a Sunday afternoon and the taste of freshly baked cookies.

In my box I will keep the smell of a Sunday dinner
And the smell of toffee pudding.

In my box I will keep the sight of a sunny day at the seaside
And the sight of the twinkling stars.

In my box I will keep the feel of a puppy's fur
And the feel of my warm and cosy bed.

My magic box closes with the feel of a warm hug from my mum!

My magic box will take me to a candyfloss land.

Gemma Lax (10)
Barnard Castle CE Primary School

My Magic Box

(Based on 'Magic Box' by Kit Wright)

My magic box is made from hard leathery dragon scales
That shine like morning stars in the sunlight
And glisten like fluorescent blue-purple flames licking the night air.
My magic box is curved like a sabre,
But pointed like a Minotaur's deadly horn,
Like stalagmites reaching for the roof of a cave
Or a peak of a mountain from afar,
Or a witch's black hat silhouetted against a clear ebony sky.

My magic box opens with a whispering sigh
And sounds like the hiss of a snake.
It opens in a cloud of mist like fog above
A field on an autumn morning.
When the hazy dew-filled mist fades away,
Inside the depths of the box lies . . .

A chicken egg and a magical ball that sparkles like stars.
It's special because it reminds me of the wonderful eclipse
And memories of my grandparents.
The mystical ball is dark deep blood-red with streaks of green
Like the colour of a green dragon scale.

My box closes like a tyre puffing out its last breath of air
And snaps shut like a dam or a Venus Flytrap
Constricting a fly in its jaw-like pincers.

Christopher Porter (10)
Barnard Castle CE Primary School

My Magic Box
(Based on 'Magic Box' by Kit Wright)

My magic box is made from a magical, sparkling, glistening
waterfall in the blazing golden sun,
with twinkling water splashing vigorously.

My magic box is the shape of a silent dove's fluffy feather,
the colour of the softest snowflake.

My magic box opens with the bleat of an innocent newborn lamb,
with a wiggle of its fluffy tail.

In my box I will keep the memories of my cousin who died,
the memories of the hottest day of the year,
the memories of crying baby eagles.

In my box I will keep the beautiful flutter of a fluttering butterfly,
the fluffy feather of a dove,
the wool of a soft woolly sheep.

In my box I will keep the taste of melting ice cream,
the lick of an excited puppy,
the kiss of a pretty angel.

In my box I will keep the purr of a kitten,
the hiss of a slithering snake,
the neigh of a frantic foal.

In my box I will keep the touch of soft, shiny, silk,
the texture of a baby's hand,
the touch of chocolate crumbling.

My box closes slowly with the buzz of a bumbling bumblebee.
In my box I will fly away to a fantasy world of fairies.

Joanna Herbert (11)
Barnard Castle CE Primary School

Rebecca's Magic Box

(Based on 'Magic Box' by Kit Wright)

My magic box is made from tender angel's wings
and superb, sparkling stars.
My magic box is the shape of freshly cried tears,
humming the sweetest sound.
My magic box opens with a flutter of fairy's wings
and a sprinkle of magic dust which smells like morning dew.
In my magic box I will keep all my treasured memories
and a touch from an angel.
I will keep afloat on a drifting, diving cloud
and a piece of the magnificent moon.
In my magic box I will keep a hug from my mum
and the tender petals from a special rose.
In my magic box I will keep a roar from the ocean
and the giggles from my friends.
In my magic box I will keep the purr from a kitten
and a bark from a dog.
In my magic box I will keep a never-ending rainbow
and my favourite dreams.
I will keep the whisper from the trees
and the feel of the refreshing breeze.
In my magic box I will keep a sparkling star
and the beautiful shining orange sunset.
In my magic box I will keep a magnificent, magical waterfall
and the cry of a newborn baby.
I will keep a caring, gentle kiss goodnight.
My magic box will close with a flash of lightning.
My magic box will take me to peaceful Heaven,
where beautiful angels sing.

Rebecca Slater (11)
Barnard Castle CE Primary School

My Magic Box
(Based on 'Magic Box' by Kit Wright)

My magic box is made from soft silk,
With eternal magic, the strongest magic ever.
My magic box is shaped like a ruby-red rosebud
With rarest diamonds on the petals.
My magic box smells like one million freshly made chocolate éclairs.
My magic box feels like the velvety feel of a cat's fur.

My magic box opens with the touch from a fluttering flying fairy.
My magic box contains the last purr from my cat,
The feel of angel's wings,
The feel of winning a competition,
The feel of swimming with the dolphins,
The song of a robin bird,
The everlasting supply of angels singing glory to the king,
Every horse in the world,
All the money ever created,
The only dragon ever existing,
The very first dinosaur,
The very first cat,
A memory from afar.

M magic box closes with the gentle, heavenly music
Slowly and quietly with a kiss from an angel
And a laugh from God.

Juliette Moore (10)
Barnard Castle CE Primary School

Plant Life Cycle

To start the cycle you need a new seed,
There are three things the desperate plant will need,
It requires water, warmth and air,
Before the tall stem appears from nowhere,
The fibrous roots will have grown as well,
No precious water will they repel,
It will absorb nutrients and water,
It does this with a hefty snorter,
When a sacred flower is produced,
To the coping plant it is a massive boost,
The healthy plant can be pollinated by insects or wind,
To juicy nectar, bees are pinned,
When the stripy bee touches the stigma
The white cell becomes a singer,
The pollen grain sinks down the never-ending tube,
The flower's coffin was overdue,
'999, come quickly please, my friends are dying.'
But it was no use trying,
The carpel grew fast and it will be
Exploding into ancient history,
The glorious seeds will be dispersed,
Important as money in a purse.

James Trevett (10)
Barnard Castle CE Primary School

These I Have Loved

These I have loved,
The hot sun shining on the lovely blue sky,
Drinking Lucozade on a lovely sunny morning,
Eating chips on the beach, going on holiday,
Seeing a clean hotel, reading a big book on a plane,
Watching plants grow,
Looking round the classroom seeing people work
And going to sleep at the end of the night, *zzzzz.*

Natalie Pettit (10)
Barnard Castle CE Primary School

My Magic Box

(Based on 'Magic Box' by Kit Wright)

My magic box is made of glistening glowing gold
And a ruby-red dragon's eye.
My magic box is shaped like a playful puppy
And a delicate wing of a beloved angel.
My magic box opens with the bark of a dopey dog
And a lightning ray from a devil's fork.
In my magic box I will keep . . .
The memories of my beautiful childhood,
The lovely sound of my jolly times,
All the shooting stars flying like a zooming comet in the night sky.

My magic box will have a red rim and a golden glow.
My magic box will fly quickly away into the night sky
And hide from sneaky intruders.
My magic box will carefully wind around my pillow
And always be there.
My magic box is only seen to my eyes
And will vanish otherwise.

My magic box closes with the laugh of a hyena
And the tear of a crying baby.

Sarah Ford (10)
Barnard Castle CE Primary School

A Look At The Ocean

Seas of emerald green on sandy shores,
Dolphins jumping joyfully through the crashing waves,
How I wish I could swim as fast as a dolphin
And see the hollow ship's bottom,
For I could see sugar-pink skies as the sun sets in summer evenings,
I wish I was a dolphin that had a lucky fin
And discover the magic world beneath the open sea
And rediscover buried treasure such as gems of sparkling dreams,
I hope that the underwater world is just exactly as it seems.

Louise Lockwood (9)
Barnard Castle CE Primary School

Magic Box

(Based on 'Magic Box' by Kit Wright)

My magic box is made from fiery metal
And the beauty of special sapphires.
My magic box is shaped like a dust dragon
With a crystal for an eye.
My magic box opens with a swing of a sword
And a shot from an arrow bursting.
In my box I will keep the one ring from the Dark Lord's finger
And the breath of my aged ancestors.

My magic box is shaped like a cat of the night
And a pink octopus.
My magic box is made of suckers from an octopus
And the breath of our great God.
In my box I will keep a golden crown and a black pearl.
My magic box opens with a click from a finger
And a bark from a dog.
My magic box closes with burning fire and a cry from a Viking raider.

Alex Salton (10)
Barnard Castle CE Primary School

If I Were . . .

If I were a flower, I would be a sweet red rose,
Cos they smell so luscious.
If I were an animal, I would be a rabbit,
Cos their fur is so soft.
If I were a bird, I would be a little robin,
Cos they sing so pleasantly.
If I were a fish, I would be a goldfish,
Cos then I could swim right up to you.
If I were a colour, I would be purple,
Cos it is perfect for me.

Laura Hackett (9)
Barnard Castle CE Primary School

Magic Box

(Based on 'Magic Box' by Kit Wright)

My magic box is made of sparkling rubies,
Precious gold and the surprise of winning the lottery.
My magic box looks like a new tube of luscious lipstick
And a colourful stained glass window.
My magic box feels like a crystal clear waterfall
And the warmth of a newborn baby's hand.
My magic box opens with the three hundred and sixty degrees
Turn of a new pair of lacy stiletto sandals
And the tick-tock of a bright pink clock.
My magic box holds in it the satisfaction of finding the one you love
And also a life supply of happiness and dazzling diamond earrings.

My magic box feels like the humiliating sting of a bee
And the feel of a piercing ear.
My magic box looks like a fluffy cloud
And a freshly brewed pint of beer.
My magic box opens with the drum of a heartbeat
And a drip of a leaking tap.
My magic box is made of the juice of a freshly squeezed orange
And a lovely tasty wine made from a tiny little grape.
My magic box holds in it the unique blink of an alien's eye
And a sigh of a tired mum.
My magic box opens with a snore from a little boy
And the tap of a tap shoe.
My magic box closes with a snappy click of a precious pen lid.

Rachel Harris (10)
Barnard Castle CE Primary School

Magic Box

(Based on 'Magic Box' by Kit Wright)

My magnificent magic box is made of the amazing, dreamy smell
Of a ruby-red rose and a sprinkling of golden fairy dust.
My magnificent magic box looks like a wisp of fine, smoky air
With a shape of a sparkling, unnoticeable diamond.
My magnificent magic box opens with a crystal teardrop falling
Gently onto the glass daisy padlock and a kiss from a beautiful
Heavenly angel.
My magnificent magic box will hold my astounding dreams,
My daily thoughts and the ghost of my late grandad.

My magnificent magic box will glow under the shining sun
And will give out goodness to the terrorised world.
My magnificent magic box will bring perfect peace
And useful understanding.
My magnificent magic box will shimmer and sleep peacefully
Under the cheesy moon.
My magnificent magic box will close gently with the smooth,
Velvety touch of a newborn baby.

Megan Lincoln (10)
Barnard Castle CE Primary School

My Magic Box

(Based on 'Magic Box' by Kit Wright)

My beautiful magic box is made of extraordinary
Clear rubies encrusted into the rich oak wood.
My wonderful box is shaped like a speeding Porsche GT3.
My magic box opens by the magnificent chant of a magical druid.
My magic box holds a mystical sword with Japanese engravings.

My magic box is made of shining gold with ivory patterns
embedded into it.
My magic box is shaped like a Samurai sword, neatly put in
its prosperous sheath.
My magic box holds the exhilarating feeling of riding on a
huge roller coaster.
My box closes by the scary roar of a sports car engine!

Michael Holder (11)
Barnard Castle CE Primary School

My Magic Box

(Based on 'Magic Box' by Kit Wright)

My magic box is made of melting Maltesers and red raw rubies.
My magic box is shaped like a dazzling diamond
Sitting on a gold ring.
My magic box opens with a sparkle of a dolphin's eye
And a click from my fingers.
In my magic box I will keep the softest touch of a dolphin's fin
And a wave of my hand.

My magic box is made of a spotted cheetah's furry coat
And a stripy zebra's skin.
My magic box is shaped like the deepest blue ocean
I have ever seen with the curliest wave ever.
My magic box will open with a twist of an old rusted key.
In my box I will keep the first smile on my face and a kick of my leg.
My magic box will close with a song from Big Brothaz'
'It Ain't What You Do'.

Kate Thompson (10)
Barnard Castle CE Primary School

Euan's Magic Box

(Based on 'Magic Box' by Kit Wright)

My magic box is made of the smell of paradise and a griffin's eye.
My magic box is shaped like an everlasting light to guide me through
my life and is shaped in peace.
My magic box opens with the click of a finger and the sound of flying
birds in the summer.
My magic box holds never-ending life and a dragon's flame.

My magic box was forged in the heavens above by the Lord's
mighty fist and hammer.
My magic box holds the spirit of Jesus and eternal praise.
My magic box was created at the same time as the Earth and
shall last forever.
My magic box closes with an owl's wing and the sound of one of my
dreams prowling the Earth.

Euan Torano (10)
Barnard Castle CE Primary School

My Magic Box

(Based on 'Magic Box' by Kit Wright)

My magic box is made of fluffy furry feathers
And curly cuddling clouds.

It shall sweetly smell like the most popular pop star perfume ever
And the shattering shape of a hopeful heart.

My magic box may open with the twinkling twist
Of a superb spectacular sparkling key.

It shall carefully keep a special touch of a dazzling dolphin
And the fuzzy feeling of the whistling wind,
The thought of shimmering sheep giving you their pretty looks.

My magic box may close as fast as a shimmering shooting star
And with the touch of a sweet-smelling flower
Gently floating and fluttering around you.

Helen Court (10)
Barnard Castle CE Primary School

Plant Life Cycle

To start the cycle a minute seed is hidden in its warm comfy lair,
To germinate it needs fresh water, warmth and air.
It starts to grow short roots,
Which anchor the thin plant like heavy boots,
They also absorb healthy nutrients and muddy water,
To make the slender stem grow from shorter to longer,
The small plant starts to grow,
But it is really slow!
The clever leaves create tasty food,
So the growing plant stays in a good mood.
The scented flower forms,
To attract the buzzing swarms,
Pollination and fertilisation - yippee
And at last comes the stripy bee.

Adam Cooper (11)
Barnard Castle CE Primary School

My Magic Box

(Based on 'Magic Box' by Kit Wright)

My magic box is made from priceless diamonds
And precious rubies from the fiery keep of the Earth.
My magic box smells like a freshly shotgun from a ravenous hunter.
My magic box looks like a dangerous great white shark
With eyes as black as death itself.
My magic box is shaped like a 1980's Harley Davidson
That reaches 100mph in a second.
My box opens with the roar from a Kawasaki 300's engine
And the sound of a dragon's deadly fire, burning forests
                                    to the ground.
In my box I will keep the keys to every motorbike in the world,
The deathly fire from a dragon's throat,
A shark from the bottom of the deep endless ocean
And the Kelton key to all toys and chocolate stores
And my box closes like a shark jumping out from the deepest sea
To catch a helpless sea lion.

Michael Brunell (11)
Barnard Castle CE Primary School

Pollination Poem

Along comes a stripy bee,
Scavenging for his nectar tea,
Flying from scented flower to colourful flower,
Looking for sweet nectar to devour,
Flying down a highly scented plant,
Sandy pollen sticks to him like an attacking ant,
Travelling to a different, beautiful flower,
For sweet nectar to devour,
The sticky pollen floats down the multicoloured plant,
Burying down the slimy style like a worker ant,
The soft eggs are fertilised and the highly aged plant starts to die,
The peapod-like carpel grows high into the wide open sky,
The microscopic seeds are dispersed from their caring mother,
Away from one or another!

Adam Dale (10)
Barnard Castle CE Primary School

Magic Box

(Based on 'Magic Box' by Kit Wright)

I will put in my box . . .
The swish of a red sari in summer moonlight
And a great ball of flamed fire
Coming from the nostrils of a Chinese dragon

I will put in my box . . .
The first time I heard a gentle whinny
From my beloved pony

I will put around my box . . .
The stars on the lid
And the deepest secrets in the corner

In my box . . .
I will have a sixth season with a black sun
A cowboy riding on a broomstick
And a witch riding on a grey horse

I will skate on my box
On high ramps with the wind blowing in my face
Then I'll tumble down and crash on the floor.

Daniel Alderson (9)
Barnard Castle CE Primary School

Things I Have Loved

These I have loved,
The artwork of artists around the world.
Cars zooming down the road
With the smell of petrol coming out the back.
The sound of dolphins in the distance of the sea.
The taste of spare ribs from the Chinese takeaway.
When I saw Jonny Wilkinson win the rugby World Cup.
When I have my family over at Christmas
And have nice meals together.
The poor army soldiers that their army made them
Go to war and take their lives away.

Bradley Layton (9)
Barnard Castle CE Primary School

Together

My dog and cat
Can sleep together,
Wherever, whenever, whatever, together.
Mum and Dad
Can walk together,
(But never when it's raining),
'That's ya mother.'
Gran and Grandad
Can sew together,
But when it's dinner time,
(They go to bed),
'That's ya 250-year-old grandad.
My dog, cat, mum, dad, gran
And grandad never
Get on all together,
Wherever, whenever, whatever,
But not together!

Kelsey Maughan (9)
Barnard Castle CE Primary School

Me

If I were a rosy-red flower
I'd be a bright red rose

If I were an octopus
I'd wave my arms around like mad

If I were a rugby player
I'd try to be as good as Jonny Wilkinson

If I were a football player
I'd try to be as good as Alan Shearer

If I were an astronaut
I'd fly to the moon.

Josh Harper (9)
Barnard Castle CE Primary School

Magic Box

(Based on 'Magic Box' by Kit Wright)

I will put in my box . . .

the breeze on a summer's day,
fairies on a fairy tree,
the feel of silk on my face.

I will put in my box . . .

a dog barking gently with her sisters,
a sip of cold water rushing down my throat,
a spark from a falling star.

I will put in my box . . .

three wishes of my own from a genie,
the last joke from an ancient grandad
and my first word.

I will put in my box . . .

a thirteenth month and a green moon,
a witch on a Hoover
and a zombie on an aeroplane.

My box is fashioned from gold string and rosemary wood,
with Yorkshire terriers around the lid
and its hinges are joints from an elephant.

I will fly on my box,
over great mountains,
then flutter back to Earth.

Mary Moore (10)
Barnard Castle CE Primary School

These I Have Loved

The luxury melted chocolate,
The kick of a football flying over your head,
Holidays when you're not at school,
My friends when they play with me,
All the juicy fruity sweets, when they melt in your mouth,
The feel of bumblebee fur when it is flying anxiously at you,
The radiant raindrops on a sunny day,
Going to the nice relaxing swimming pool,
Having a bath on an icy day,
My PlayStation 2 on football,
Making sandcastles on holiday,
Aeroplanes when they are going very fast,
New aftershave on Christmas Day,
Christmas Day when you retrieve things from Santa.

James Thwaites (9)
Barnard Castle CE Primary School

These I Have Loved

The kick of a football flying across the swift, crispy grass,
The hot sun thirsty, piercing down my pale shadowy skin,
Luxury chocolate melting like leaves,
Trembling down a hard tree trunk,
Dogs barking like rapid arguments
Appearing though it feels calm,
Holidays when you get to miss school
And do anything you like,
The smell of hissing makes me feel
Like flower petals smelling delicious,
Going swimming when you get to relax softly
In a nice sweet corner,
Drawing pictures of nasty wolves
Or even sweet little girls.

Philip Merryweather (9)
Barnard Castle CE Primary School

If I Were . . .

If I were a monkey, I would be a chimpanzee,
Cos they jump branch to branch.

If I were a great white shark,
I would soar the seas all over the block.

If my dad was a fuzzy fox,
He'd be running from shooting guns.

If my dad was a kangaroo,
He'd be jumping around Australia.

If my mum was a beautiful dove,
She'd be flying over the pub.

If my mum was a furry cat,
She'd climb trees round the shop.

Jordan Thompson Parkin (10)
Barnard Castle CE Primary School

I'll Follow You

I'll follow you
In the door
Under the dense carpet
In the greasy kitchen
In the sizzling pans
Around the slimy wet plughole
To the depths of the long carpet
Up the jagged staircase
In the blue bedroom
Along the grand oak bed
In the soft silky bed
By the burning hot radiator
Down the stairs
And out of the door.

Joseph Brown (10)
Barnard Castle CE Primary School

Rainbows

R uby-red
A ll mixed up
I t's indigo
N othing happening
B oring blue
O pen up, it's orange
W hen the sun's out it's . . .
S ilver, ruby-red, blue, orange, indigo, green, yellow, purple,
   violet and pink.

Alice Wood (9)
Barnard Castle CE Primary School

Summer

S ummer is the warmest month,
U nited States left behind,
M oney is spent, with people going on holiday,
M ajorca, America, Australia, people going there,
E verybody sunbathing, boiling on the head,
R ound and round again, little people getting stung.

Stacey Walker (7)
Barnard Castle CE Primary School

Is . . .

Is a rainbow a bow that rains?
Is a goalpost a post that scores a goal?
Is a goldfish a fish shaped like a piece of gold?
Is a caveman a man who's in a cave?
Is a great grandma, a grandma who's really big?
Is a football a foot shaped like a ball?
Is a crack the crack in an earthquake?

Robert Mounter (8)
Barnard Castle CE Primary School

Try! Try! Try!

T ake a chance,
R eally concentrate,
Y ou can do it,
I f you try, you could,
N ever give up,
G o and see what you can do.

H eave the rope
A nd grip on with your feet,
R eally good,
D on't stop!
E xcellent, you're nearly there,
R ebecca! You're at the very top!
   Can you climb a mountain?
   Well *try!*

Rebecca Watson (9)
Barnard Castle CE Primary School

Lights

Lights shine bright,
Lights bring delight.

Lights glow,
Lights flow.

Lights crash,
Lights flash,
Lights just fade away.

Lights are shiny,
Lights are mostly tiny.

Lights dazzle,
Lights gleam,
Lights are glossy.

Fiona Cook (9)
Barnard Castle CE Primary School

Books Are . . .

Books are history, literacy,
Numeracy, science,
All books are fantastic.

Shaped books, long books,
Straight books, curly books,
Furry books, all kinds of fantastic books.

Some books are thin,
Books with pictures,
Books, dictionary, books.

Kieran Briggs (8)
Barnard Castle CE Primary School

Ponies

Ponies are brill!
Ponies can gallop,
Ponies run like the wind,
Ponies are interesting,
Ponies feel magical,
Ponies conjure up a whole new world,
Ponies sense what you feel like,
Ponies are fun,
Ponies are good.

Emily Bonnett (9)
Barnard Castle CE Primary School

School Is . . .

School is a place to learn.
School is a place with friends.
School is anyone's nightmare.
School is a place to think.
School is a terrible place.
School is an educational place.

Craig Torano (8)
Barnard Castle CE Primary School

What Is Yellow?

What is yellow?
Yellow is a banana lying in the sun,
Yellow is a ball of fire in the air,
Yellow is the sun blazing hot,
Yellow is fire lit on a match,
Yellow is a yellow jumper hanging up,
Yellow is a book someone is writing in,
Yellow is a crayon, the brightest in the box,
Yellow is sand on the beach, children playing having fun!

Amy Tones (8)
Barnard Castle CE Primary School

Red

Red is the colour of my spelling book
Red is a popular colour
Red is the colour of the Devil
Red can make you angry
Red is the colour of sadness
Red is a hot place
Red can burn you
Red is the colour of Mrs Pollard's jumper
Red is my mum's favourite colour.

Isobel Thomas (8)
Barnard Castle CE Primary School

Sharks

Sharks live in the sea
They might eat you
And they might eat me
They like to eat meat
So you shouldn't look neat
Or wear lots of blue
Because they might eat you.

Rory Lincoln (7)
Barnard Castle CE Primary School

Colours

Blue is the colour of the sea
Dancing very happily.
White is the colour of the snow
That lays on the ground and brightly glows.
Green is the colour of the grass
Swaying in the breeze quite fast.
Red is the colour of your heart
Just like a lovely big jam tart.
Black is the colour of the dark night sky
Getting ready to pass by.

Lauren Smith (9)
Barnard Castle CE Primary School

Fire

Fire burning, everybody out
People running all about

Fire blazing all the night
Firefighters have to fight

Families darting to the sea
Animals want to flee.

Edward Harding (8)
Barnard Castle CE Primary School

Rainbows

R ainbow colours full of glee,
A mber orange you can see,
I like the lavender best of all,
N ow you can see all colours,
B ut you never see black or brown,
O h no, it goes away,
W hat a lovely sight I see,
S o everyone remembers it.

Bryony Gargett (8)
Barnard Castle CE Primary School

Blue

Blue is sky
Blue is the colour of bluebells
Blue is tears falling from your eyes
Blue is the rain falling from the clouds
Blue is the colour of water
Blue is sadness
Blue is cold
Blue is the colour of the classroom
Blue is the dark of night
Blue is my favourite colour.

Lucy Scott (9)
Barnard Castle CE Primary School

Summer

Summer is fun and laughter,
Mum and Dad and little daughter,
In the park they have picnics
And make fires out of sticks.
In the sun they will play,
There will be happiness all day,
When it starts to grow colder,
They will go home to have supper.

Jessica Moore (7)
Barnard Castle CE Primary School

Sun

The sun is bright,
The sun is light,
It might be tight,
The sun is not white,
It's only asleep at night.

Amy Lowson (7)
Barnard Castle CE Primary School

Wind!

Wind is a breeze across your face,
Wind is a thing that blows your lace,
Wind is a blow from above,
Wind is a kiss of God's love,
Wind is a wave of someone's hand,
Wind is a trumpet from a band,
Wind is a blow of cold air from a fan,
Wind is steam from a pan,
Wind is the breath of a dragon,
Wind is air from the back of a wagon,
Wind is us running in a race,
Wind, why do you blow on my face?

Natalie Hobson (9)
Barnard Castle CE Primary School

Weather

Weather is sometimes bad,
Because it makes you mad.
When it is sunny,
It is quite runny,
Just like honey.
Honey is scrumming.
The rain is dropping,
As raindrops are knocking,
Soon the people will open the door
And start stomping on the floor.
They soon get thrown out of the house
And get tickled by a woodlouse.

Jennifer Healy (8)
Barnard Castle CE Primary School

Things I Like

I like dogs - they are like cuddly toys
I like sausages - they are delicious and crunchy
I like the beach - it's hot and fun
I like the sun - it's a beautiful yellow
I like milk - it's white and sweet
I like cows - they give you milk
I like my rabbit - it's sweet and cuddly
I like rice - it's nice with curry
I like discos - you can dance at them
I like the sea - it's fun to swim
I like swimming - it gives me energy
I like Mum - she cooks wonderful food
I like school - you go on good school trips
I like birthdays - they're exciting and cool.

Shannon Toole (10)
Barnard Castle CE Primary School

Images

If I was a colour, I would be lush lilac.
If I was a piece of furniture, I would be a lounge bed.
If I was music, I would be Black Eyed Peas.
If my brother was a building, he would be the Eiffel Tower.
If my brother was music, he would be Eminem.
If my brother was food, he would be pizza.
If my nana was music, she would be UB40.
If my nana was furniture she would be an armchair.
If my nana was a colour she would be yellow.
If my dad was weather, he would be snow.
If my dad was a season, he would be winter.
If my dad was a plant, he would be a bush.

Samantha Berry (9)
Barnard Castle CE Primary School

Pollination Poem

Look over there, there's a stripy bee,
I hope he's coming here for his nectar tea,
I am a tall flower that smells really nice,
Yellow bees really like me, they don't think twice,
If you look at my red petals, they are very bright,
They would not be here if there was no light!

Look at that stripy bee,
He is going to pollinate me,
The pollen on his little belly,
Will go into the he ovary,
When the sticky pollen goes down the oval style,
My tiny eggs will then be fertile,
Everything will then suddenly die
And the seed holding carpel will grow towards the blue sky,
The green carpel will grow and grow
And eventually it will blow!

Jake Gargett (10)
Barnard Castle CE Primary School

Snow Is . . .

Snow is as cold as ice,
White as can be.

Snow is full of joy
And people make snowmen.

Snow is no more hot summer,
But lots of cold winter.

Snow is cold and windy,
The north wind blows when it snows.

Snow is Santa
And presents for Christmas.

Jack Holguin (8)
Barnard Castle CE Primary School

Images

I'd rather be salt than pepper.
I'd rather be a girl than a boy.
I'd rather be rich than poor.
I'd rather be thin than fat.
I'd rather be a finger than a thumb.
I'd rather be light than dark.
I'd rather be a pen than a pencil.
I'd rather be a table than a chair.
I'd rather be a cup than a saucer.
I'd rather be a sun than a moon.
I'd rather be a sock than a shoe.
I'd rather be a mum than a dad.
I'd rather be high than low.
I'd rather be a number than a letter.
I'd rather be clear than foggy.
I'd rather be a rubber than a ruler.
I'd rather be gold than silver.
I'd rather be brave than afraid.

Charlotte Dye (9)
Barnard Castle CE Primary School

Cars

Cars are fast
Cars are bright
Cars shine in the moonlit night

Cars are new
Cars are old
Cars have seats that can fold

Cars are sporty
Cars are racing
Cars are chasing.

Ian Bell (9)
Barnard Castle CE Primary School

Think Rainbow

Think of red,
What is red?
Red is the cover
Of my own soft bed.

Think of orange,
What is orange?
Orange is the colour
Of an orange of course!

Think of yellow,
What is yellow?
Yellow is a pear,
Cool and mellow.

Think of green,
What is green?
Green is the face
Of a monster mean.

Think of blue,
What is blue?
Blue is the polish
On a warm soft shoe.

Think of indigo,
What is indigo?
Indigo is valleys
From a cloud of snow.

Think of violet,
What is violet?
Violet are the mountains
From the view of a pilot.

Alice Carr (9)
Barnard Castle CE Primary School

My Magic Box

(Based on 'Magic Box' by Kit Wright)

My magic box is made of crystal wood
With chocolate, strawberry and vanilla ice cream

My magic box looks like a hamster with sharp teeth
And a little small tail

My magic box is shaped like a ten pound note

My magic box smells like a stink bomb going off onto the floor

My magic box opens like a angel singing a prayer to God

In my box I will keep a photo of me and Miss Savory eating ice cream
And a photo of me, my dad and my mum and also me and Mr Lees

My magic box closes like a dragon breathing breath of hot fire.

Sarah Hanson (10)
Barnard Castle CE Primary School

Things I Have Loved

The cracking and crunching of a cucumber's first bite,
The crying and the soft fur of a cat,
The barking and the fast legs of a dog,
The volume and the picture of a TV,
The lying and relaxing of a sofa,
The comfortable feeling when I jump into a chair,
The lying under the covers and curling up in bed,
The water dribbling down the side of my face,
The tick and the tock of a clock,
The swaying and swinging of a door,
The engine of a car revving up to 100 mile an hour.

Robert Dixon (9)
Barnard Castle CE Primary School

Things I Like

The smooth calm music of Westlife.
The chewy cheese of crunchy pizzas.
The delicious smell of salty soft chips.
The luxurious brown leather sofas.
The shimmering silver jewellery of a princess.
The cutest most cuddly teddy.
The sweet smell of flowers in the springtime.
The playful soft white snow in the wintertime.
The shimmering of the stars at night.
The bright mysterious gleaming moon at night.
The calm colour of lilac.
The cool splashes from wet dolphins' tails.
The baby lambs in springtime, leaping across the hilltops.
The biggest, most comfortable, most bouncy bed.

Danielle Cassidy (9)
Barnard Castle CE Primary School

Images

If I were a colour I would be glittering gold.
If I were a building I would be Man Utd's football stadium.
If I were music I would be Busted.

If my brother were weather he would be snow.
If my brother was a piece of furniture he would be a white leather sofa.
If my brother were a season he would be winter.

If my dad were a season he would be spring.
If my dad were a food he would be a hot curry.
If my dad were music he would be a ballad.

If my mum were a colour she would be sparkling silver.

Jonathan Foster (9)
Barnard Castle CE Primary School

Love And Hate

I love my room because the sun hits the window.
The thing I hate about my room is when it starts to rain.
I love my brother because he always tidies my room up.
The thing I hate about my brother is that he messes my room up.
I like my mum because she makes nice desserts.
I hate my dog because he slobbers everywhere.
I love my dog because he is always sleeping next to the fire.
I hate my sisters because they are very nasty.
I love my dad because he always fixes my toys.
I hate my chimney because it smells and it is very old.
I love my school because my teachers are very funny!
I hate my brother because he plays with my toys and breaks them.
I love my school because we get lots of homework.
I hate my homework because we get too much of it.
I love my garden because it is like a park and it has a conker tree in it.
The thing I hate about my garden is when it rains.
I love my room because it is bright and it has lots of toys.

Ben Ball (11)
Barnard Castle CE Primary School

Things I Like

The crispy bacon roll is like a crunchy leaf of an autumn day.
The soft fur of a dog is like a ball of straw.
The hard football is like a brick wall.
The spike of a dart is like a point of a pen.
The loud rock music is like all the pop bands.
The loud war machine is like a building falling down.
The loud rush of a motorbike is like a chainsaw cutting down a tree.
The fast racing car is like a cheetah running.
The hot pepperoni is like a fiery oven.

Adam Black (10)
Barnard Castle CE Primary School

My Magic Box

(Based on 'Magic Box' by Kit Wright)

My magic box is made from the best of all jewels,
Encrusted with my favourite things.

My magic box is shaped like a leaping dog
Courageously fighting the greatest of his fears
As I feel gaiety in abundance from it all.

My magic box opens with the sound of guilty armies' roar
Gracefully saving me from danger, making me feel like royalty.

In my magic box I will keep the key to every door,
The amusement I've never seen,
The purpose of my living,
Every wish of my dreams,
The excitement I've ever wanted,
My magic box holds only my things.

My magic box closes with the swish of a silvery key,
The one and only key,
Glinting in the moonlight, but only on my accord.

On my box I will fly the seven seas,
Eternally my box is unique to me.

Jamie Holder (11)
Barnard Castle CE Primary School

Snow

The snow is cold,
The snow is white,
The snow is fun,
The snow is light,
The snow is liquid,
The snow is for snowmen,
The snow is very bright,
The snow is just so much . . . fun!
We want it.

Harley Oliver (7)
Barnard Castle CE Primary School

Things That I Love

Small country cottages covered in crawling vines, dropping shiny leaves.
Realistic pictures laden with paint and life, ready for eyes to lay upon them.
Complicated math sums written on a blackboard waiting to be answered on a piece of paper.
Soft squishy beds, plump and warm, smooth and totally untouched.
Dew-covered blue and red specks laid around flowery, small lovely forest.
Shapeless cotton wool-like clouds forming different things in the sky above us.
Clear turquoise sky ready for a plane to fly by.
Everlasting, silent, untouched snow upon a timid country house.
New, sweet books smelling of woods and magical adventures.
Bright, growing colours lighting up rooms and lives.
Flowing fountain pens gliding across the page like feathers in the wind.

Elisabeth Harding (10)
Barnard Castle CE Primary School

Things I Have Liked

I like the morning heat of the sun's rays,
I like the soft little flakes of snow that flutter about in the winter nights.
I like the tiny, transparent drops of water falling from the sky.
I like the glinting shine of my brand new mountain bike.
I like the golden strings of everlasting spaghetti Bolognese.
I like the hot stringy cheese from the tomato and cheese pizzas.
I like the loud echoing cheers and shouts from football games.
I like the laughing noise of gurgling fresh water from
                          the high mountains.
I like the new gentle winds of spring.
I like the interesting wet rustling noise of people kicking the
                          fallen autumn leaves.

Matthew Bainbridge (10)
Barnard Castle CE Primary School

Magic Box

(Based on 'Magic Box' by Kit Wright)

My magic box is made of glinting gold and gruesome ghost.
My box is shaped like an athlete James Milner with a singing
sparrow on top.
My box opens with the sound of a mighty blizzard thrashing down
and the bark of a black Labrador dog.
In my box I will keep the lazy feeling of being in my cosy bed for the
last minute before getting up for a hot gravy-filled Yorkshire pudding.

My magic box is made of dazzling diamonds and crimson red rubies.
My box is shaped like a huge shiny treasure chest with a
twinkling decoration.
My box opens with the wail of a huge killer whale leaping in the sea air
and the superb atmosphere of a cracking football match.
In my box I will keep the world's best trained dog and the only 106
wheeler artic wagon in the world.
My box closes slowly with the sound of the bagpipes.

Matthew Brough (11)
Barnard Castle CE Primary School

Love And Hate

The thing I love about the sun is its lovely warmth.
The thing I hate about the sun is becoming badly burnt.
The thing I love about summer is developing nice tans.
The thing I hate about summer is all the devilish bees.
The thing I love about a Lamborghini is its fantastic speed.
The thing I hate about a Lamborghini is its small boot.
The thing I love about a Ferrari is its loud roar from its engine.
The thing I hate about a Ferrari is its very ugly doors.
The thing I love about football is always winning a trophy.
The thing I hate about football is always unluckily loosing.
The thing I love about cheetahs is their fantastic speed.
The thing I hate about cheetahs is their strange tails.
The thing I love about running is always winning.
The thing I hate about running is always falling over.

Andrew Scott (11)
Barnard Castle CE Primary School

Images Of Me

I'd rather be a giraffe than a crocodile.
I'd rather be a cup than a saucer.
I'd rather have tomato sauce than brown sauce.
I'd rather have water than a fizzy drink.
I'd rather be low than high.
I'd rather be a ball than a bat.
I'd rather be cold than hot.
I'd rather write with pen than pencil.
I'd rather drink than eat.
I'd rather be empty than full.
I'd rather be clean than dirty.
I'd rather be in rain than sun.
I'd rather be in snow than wind.
I'd rather be left out in the light than left out in the dark.
I'd rather be rich than poor.
I'd rather be small than big.
I'd rather save up than spend everything.
I'd rather be asleep than awake.
I'd rather have long hair than have short hair.
I'd rather have big nails than short nails.
I'd rather be popular than lonely.
I'd rather have a friend than not.
I'd rather have a boyfriend than not have one.

Paige Wilkinson (9)
Barnard Castle CE Primary School

Purple

Purple is fun and kind
In the breeze he looks behind
In the funny purple eyes he says,
'That's mine so look behind'
Purple is lots of joy in the sky or in *me!*
Everyone sees purple but he says, 'Go Mr Turtle'
Purple is a lovely thing, mean or happy
But he just wanted to say, 'It's purple day today.'

Sarah Teasdale (8)
Barnard Castle CE Primary School

Things I Love

The soft shine of gold sparkling
The joy of playing with my toys
A boiling hot breakfast of beans on toast
A luxurious soft bed to sleep in
Programmes that go on all day and night on TV
A rugby tackle that makes you ache
The sun that shines and the sandcastle that you make
Seawater to surf on through the waves
A fire burning in the moonlight
Scary stories with bats in the night
The water rushing in a river, unlike a stream
Being part of a home rugby team
Throwing snowballs at my dad
And it's annoying when he's mad
The smell of flowers in the forest . . .

Liam Brown (9)
Barnard Castle CE Primary School

Playing

Do you like saying,
'Hey, come on, let's go and play'?

Everybody's outside,
Oh, please let me on the slide!

Shall we go on the swing
Before my eyes really sting?

Oh why do you have to nag me?
Look! Mum's calling you for tea.

Natalie Garner (7)
Barnard Castle CE Primary School

My Family

My auntie's going crazy
My uncle's got the flu
Mum's running round and round wondering what to do

My dad goes to work
My nana bakes the food
My sister just sits there, always in a mood

My brother always teases me
My cousin goes to school
And me, I just relax, sitting in my swimming pool.

Rachel Tunstall (10)
Dodmire Junior School

Waterfall

It comes charging down
With spray shooting upwards
Clattering onto the rocks
On its way to the sea
The splashing water gleams
When it's whipping up the foam
Over the rocks wildly
While it's rushing down
Oh what a wonderful sight.

Philip Stephenson (10)
Dodmire Junior School

Snail

Shimmering silver trail
Left behind by the sluggish snail
Slowly, silently making his lazy way
Round shady, secret places
In the garden.

Jordan Green (9)
Dodmire Junior School

Waterfall

W hooshing wildly
A wesome to my eyes
T reetops get a soaking
E ventually reaching the sea
R ushing and hurrying
F alling majestically
A ll the water tumbling down
L oudly crashing
L ively journey, down and down.

Natasha Bennett (9)
Dodmire Junior School

Waterfall

W ater helplessly falling
A mazing and outstanding
T remendous and fantastic
E ffortlessly plunging to the pool below
R oaring
F lowing as fast as a cheetah
A s wild as a lion
L ively, rushing flow
L iving water.

David Freak (10)
Dodmire Junior School

My Family

There is Richard my stepdad, he's mad
There is Kath my auntie, she's a bit of a laugh
Then there is Sue, she likes a bit of a brew
And there's Cris, who is a Rangers fan, oh what a sad man
Of course my mother, I wouldn't have any other.

Thomas Taylor (10)
Dodmire Junior School

Snail

Garden snail
Drags himself
Through green, prickly bushes
On to damp stone walls
Leaving behind
A slippery, slimy trail
Gripping his foot fast
On mossy walls
Pulling himself
Sluggishly along
Silently
A w a y
And
A w a y
Until he is out of sight.

Abbie Luck (9)
Dodmire Junior School

The Waterfall Poem

The waterfall, the deadly waterfall
Rushing over the pebbles and rocks
Light chasing the moving rapids
Dodging huge fossils and bones
It slowly curves for the fall of its afterlife
Down
Down
Down
Falls the waves of the dead
Suddenly crashing like explosions
Of minefields
Finally flowing gently to the ocean.

Luke Swannell (9)
Dodmire Junior School

Playing Football

Men shooing,
 Fans whistling,
  Keepers shouting,
   Ref arguing,
     Defenders tackling,
      Captains scoring,
       Shots thumping,
        Floodlights gleaming,
        Strikers diving,
        Fans groaning,
         Liverpool winning,
         Everton losing,
          Mascots dancing,
           Whistle screeching,
           Managers sighing.

Nicholas Wiper (9)
Dodmire Junior School

Waterfall

W hooshing water
A waterfall zooms furiously down
T remendous and splashing
E xciting
R oaring downwards
F alling and cascading
A n outstanding view
L ovely and glittering
L ively water.

Caramon Collinson (9)
Dodmire Junior School

Up In The Attic

(and . . . something . . . stirring)
        an old doll with ringlets
        a chest of drawers (again, they were rotting)
        an old wooden rotting chair
        a portrait of the family
        a rocking horse with woodworm
        a dusty navy dancing dress
        an old brush infested with hair
        cans of beer (rusting)
        dirty metal pipes
        old work files
        planks of dusty old wood
        bags of ancient clothes
        old photo albums
Up in the attic

Olivia Johnson (10)
Dodmire Junior School

Waterfall

W hooshing, swooshing
A massive sight
T hrashing, banging, crashing
E nergetic
R acing
F iercely falling
A ll the way down
L ively
L iving water.

Conor Davies (10)
Dodmire Junior School

My Dog, Barney

Barney is my dog
He likes to play in the park
Sleeps like a log
And eats faster than his bark

Watch out in the bath
He'll follow you
Watch your path
Or he'll like you too.

Jessica Elve (10)
Dodmire Junior School

Football

Players shooting
  Fans hooting
    Defenders tackling
      Midfielder crossing
        Referee whistling
          Attackers booting
            Post rattling
              Fans fighting.

Corey Aldus (9)
Dodmire Junior School

Waterfall

Whooshing wildly
Down and down
Its sparkling water will surprise you
Flowing without a care
Racing
Rushing rapidly
Falling noisily
Ever downwards.

Annastasia Wade (9)
Dodmire Junior School

The Months Of The Year

January brings the snow,
Makes my toes tingle and glow.
February brings the rain,
Floods the grounds down the lane.
March brings breezes loud and shrill,
Stirs the dancing daffodil.
April brings the primrose sweet,
Scatters daisies at my feet.
May brings floods of pretty lambs,
Skipping around their fleecy mams.
June brings tulips, lilies and roses,
The scents of smells go up our noses.
Hot July brings cooling showers,
Jelly with ice cream and beautiful flowers.
August brings the sheaves of corn,
Then the harvest home is borne.
Warm September brings the fruit,
Sportsmen then begin to shoot.
Fresh October brings the pheasant,
Gathering nuts is very pleasant.
Dull November brings the blast,
Then the leaves are falling fast.
Chilly December brings the sleet,
Blazing fire and Christmas treat.

Susan Sung (11)
Dodmire Junior School

Flowers!

Flowers are the life of spring,
When the birds coo and sing.

Flowers are the colours on the ground,
When the bees buzz and make a silly sound.

Flowers are the colours of winter,
When the white rosebuds glinter.

Rebecca-Naomi Littlefair (11)
Dodmire Junior School

The Magic Mirror

Look into the magic mirror,
Come find what you can see,
Could it be a brand new bike
Or simply you and me?

Could it be a castle,
High in the sky?
Could it be a happy clown
Or delicious apple pie?

Could it be a pretty bow
Or birds among the trees
Or could it be a wicked queen
With awful knobbly knees?

Could it be a smelly pig
Or flowers in the park
Or could it be a nasty dog
Just about to bark?

So look into the magic mirror,
Find out what you can see,
Could it be a brand new bike
Or simply you and me?

Natalie Winter (11)
Dodmire Junior School

The Waterfall

Firing down at high speeds
A lot of water is all it needs
Crashing down on all the rocks
Each time it hits, it gives little knocks
Shining sparkly white
It will be such a sight
But there are surprises hidden inside
Almost as bad as the tide
If you go to jump, just wait
Because it might just be your fate

Benjamin Snowball (9)
Dodmire Junior School

My Cousin's Horse, Bobby

My cousin's horse, Bobby pulls a cart
My cousin's horse, Bobby looks smart
My cousin's horse, Bobby is the best
Only when he has a rest

When my cousin wants Bobby to go faster
He says, 'Giddy up Bobby!'

My cousin's horse loves to pace
And he loves to have a race

When we put him into the stable
He runs like mad to get his hay

My cousin's horse, Bobby is as quiet as a lamb
He loves to get washed
And he loves to get brushed

That's my cousin's horse, Bobby.

Robert Ward (10)
Dodmire Junior School

At The Bottom Of My Bed!

You don't want to know what's at the bottom of my bed,
There's two smelly goldfish,
One is called Fred.

There are rotten socks
And vile smells,
There is even a rusty golden bell.

Nobody dares to come in my room,
Because at the bottom of my bed,
It is doom and gloom.

Susan Glew (11)
Dodmire Junior School

Seasons

S un shining
P ink blossoms
R ich chocolate
I nteresting flowers
N ights shorter
G reen leaves

S un shimmering
U ltraviolet
M ums stressed
M onstrous offers
E nding holidays
R ivers flowing

A ugust has gone
U mbrellas being used
T rees losing leaves
U sing conkers
M oney being spent
N ever-ending leaves

W ine being drank
I nteresting snow
N o leaves
T rees bare
E verlasting ice
R oads dangerous.

Tegan Stevenson (9)
Dodmire Junior School

The Snail

A slow snail
Leaves his trail
On the wet day
The little sparkly, spiky, black eyes
The only place he has to live is his
Curly
Whirly
Swirly
Pearly shell
Where he can hide away from danger and
Attack!

Georgina Wade (9)
Dodmire Junior School

Football Poem

Nana's in goal
Uncle's in defence
Mother's in midfield
Dad's on the bench
Auntie's in attack
Grandad is the manager
And just because
I missed a penalty
I'm on the free transfer list.

Jack Littlefair (8)
Dodmire Junior School

The Butterfly

Fluttering
Delicate
Collecting nectar
The beautiful butterfly.

Alanna Stevenson (7)
Dodmire Junior School

Waterfall

Smashing off the rock
Like it's pouring with rain, thunder and lighting.
Taking everything down
In its strong current.
Wild salmon and trout jump up.
At the bottom of the waterfall
Lies a pond full of fish.
The air is covered by a huge white cloud,
The waterfall flows into a nice calm river.

Stephen Richardson (10)
Dodmire Junior School

My Teacher

My teacher is always telling me, 'Watch what you write,
You'd better stop that chattering else I'll keep you here all night,
You'd better stop swinging on that chair, you'll have a nasty fall,
Jack, put down your pencil and step back from that wall.'
She's always moaning, never stops and rests,
Once she really lost her temper and called us all little pests.
We all love our teacher, we think she's the best in the school,
She spends loads of time with us, which we think is really cool!

Kathryn Woolston (11)
Dodmire Junior School

The Big Black Cat

I was crossing the road the other day,
When I heard a noise,
I turned around, there was nothing there,
Until I saw . . . *the big black cat!*
Who was very, very fat with a big long tail.

Nathaniel Wilson (8)
Dodmire Junior School

The Storm

Lightning strikes and off it goes
Leaving woodland an fiery glow
The sky darkens and gets very black
Is this the lightning coming back?

When the rain comes falling down
That's what makes the floods
Then lightning strikes and burns some houses
Houses burn down and fall on the street
The cars get stuck in floods and crash
Into the side of the road.

Jason Watt (7)
Dodmire Junior School

The Waterfall

It splashes, clashes and thrashes as it hits the rocks below,
It booms the water onto the messy rocks,
It showers, it sprays, it soaks everything that's in its way,
From little rapids to big waterfalls,
Their currents can be deadly,
Underneath the water there's the black pit with dangerous rocks,
You can drown in this waterfall,
No matter what they do, you can't get back up.

Hayley Jemmett (10)
Dodmire Junior School

Girly Spell

Take a fairy's wing
Hear the pixie sing
Add to two drops of love
And a sparkling ring
To make that boy go totally crazy.

Tallia Cornforth (10)
Dodmire Junior School

Football Girl

There is a girl in ball class
She did pass, she did pass
I do not know why, but she does good
I wish I could, I wish I could

She won the cup, she won the cup
And with the money she bought a pup
She scored some goals
By kicking balls, in she bowls

It makes me mad, it makes me mad
That I do bad, that I do bad
So now I go to learn ball class
For some reason they let me pass.

Sophie Pursey (8)
Dodmire Junior School

The Waterfall

The waterfall is sparkling in the distance
It is so magical
You can see right through it
The waterfall might be beautiful
But it can be very dramatic indeed
Black holes, dark caves
And pits full of rocks
I can't imagine what it would be like
If you fell into it
It wouldn't be so beautiful then
Washed away in the dark swirling water
Dangerous wonders in this wonderful sight.

Andrew Pitt (10)
Dodmire Junior School

When I Hug My Baby

When I hug my baby
When she starts to cry
Then I hug my baby
She starts to sigh
When I hug my baby
She's so cute
When I hug my baby
In her baby suit
When I don't hug my baby
She gets upset
But then I think, *I know . . .*
I'll get her a pet.

Chelsea McIntyre (8)
Dodmire Junior School

The Waterfall

The waterfall whooshes and splashes
When the water falls it flies through the air
When it hits the floor it is like an earthquake
And starts to foam like angry bulls
The spray hits you and you are very wet
The crashing and splashing of the waterfall.

Liam Greaves (9)
Dodmire Junior School

Playing Football

Middlesbrough scoring
 Crowds yawning
  Chelsea winning
   People singing
    Whistle blowing
     Everyone going.

Heather Smith-Burns (8)
Dodmire Junior School

The Waterfall Breeze

Splash, splash
Clashing the waterfall
With clouds of misty spray
Splash, splash
Tumbling waterfall
Thrashing the rocky cascade
Splash, splash
Rumbles the waterfall
Hitting every rock
Splash, splash
Rippling waterfall
In the moonlight
Splash, splash
Energetic waterfall
You are an amazing sight.

Jack Tenwick (9)
Dodmire Junior School

Friends Forever

B est friends forever
E specially with Jo
S at next to each other in class
T ea together round mine

F riends for eternity
R ely on each other all the time
I deal friends in our minds
E njoy each other's company
N ever-ending friendship
D elightful friends all the time
S leepovers round each other's houses.

Laura Nickson (9)
Dodmire Junior School

My Mind's Thoughts

My life is very strange
It's not what it seems
I often think of things
That have no real means
Like the breath of the sea
Turning into lions' roars
Whooshing in my face
Like repelling doors
I dream of giant castles
That have stood proud and bold
And after many years
Still don't look old
I wonder what it's like
To touch a dragon's wing
Or maybe see a troll
That hopelessly tries to sing
But what I really want
More than the whole world
Is to travel everywhere
Making the greatest story told.

Lewis McIntyre (10)
Dodmire Junior School

Sunshine

S hining bright
U nder the fluffy clouds
N eatly placed
S himmering in the blue sky
H anging high and bright
 I n the deep, deep sky
N ever-ending sunlight
E very day it shines
   Sunshine!

Louise Chapman (9)
Dodmire Junior School

The Bill

There is a TV show called The Bill
Where the people work at Sun Hill
There's people called Guv and Sarge
They're the ones who are in charge
It's got bad people who rob and steal
But the police have handcuffs made of steel
They lock the bad guys away
And do this day after day.

Andrew Elliott (10)
Dodmire Junior School

Waterfall

Whooshing and whirling
An amazing sight
Tremendous body of water
Eating away at the rocks
Rushing rhythmically
At an astonishing pace
A fantastic sight
That will leave you flabbergasted.

George Ward (10)
Dodmire Junior School

Snail

Slowly and leisurely creeps the garden snail,
Pulling itself along on one shaky foot.
Noiselessly it slithers along,
Making slow progress along the bumpy, gravely path.
All behind leaving a silvery trail,
Glinting in the moonlight.

James Cooke (10)
Dodmire Junior School

Waterfall

W aterfall flashing down
A great view
T remendous
E normous splash
R oaring wildly
F alling loudly
A whoosh of a noise
L ovely, glittering water
L ively and loud.

Richard Sung (10)
Dodmire Junior School

Waterfall

The waterfall tumbles violently
Head over heels
Tremendous and outstanding
Falling into the dark pool below
Splashing and spraying water
Cascading rapidly
Down to the bottom
Crashing, splashing
It takes your breath away.

Sarah Bamber (9)
Dodmire Junior School

Waterfall

Charging downwards
The waterfall looks alive
Splashing into the gloomy water below
Falling rapidly
Blinding spray
What a view!

Jonathan Robinson (10)
Dodmire Junior School

Waterfall

Vast body of water
Flowing over rough, ragged rock
Amazing
Awesome
Water flying over the edge
Terrific bubbling foam
As it crashes down
Everlasting
Never stopping
Always rushing
Racing down
Sounds like thunder
Always crashing and splashing
Fierce torrents
Thrashing furiously against the rocks
Astonishing
Cascading
Lively and dangerous
Forceful
Living and roaring
Racing and changing.

Anthony Watt (10)
Dodmire Junior School

Waterfall

W onderful
A mazing
T errible
E xciting
R oaring
F alling
A stounding
L oud
L iving water.

Graeme Briggs (10)
Dodmire Junior School

The Wind Howls, The Wind Blows

The wind howls, the wind blows,
The storm continues, the river flows.
Trees creak, bend and snap,
Then thunder echoes with a clap
And the wind howls, the wind blows.

Then everything shakes and clatters,
All around is in tatters.
It wasn't on the weather forecast,
Oh no! Another great blast!
And the wind howls, the wind blows.

Then there is a great big glow,
As lightning strikes and puts on a show.
It comes with a flash, a huge crack,
Makes me want to hide or pack
And the wind howls, the wind blows.

Michaela Mullett (8)
Dodmire Junior School

Waterfall

W ater swishes down very fast
A wesome, steaming rush
T errifying sight
E xtremely cold
R acing like a bright band of ribbon
F alling rapidly
A mazing
L isten to the splashing and cracking
L ight spray shoots into the air.

Amy Sung (9)
Dodmire Junior School

The Sun Rises, The Sun Falls

The sun rises, the sun falls,
The sky gets dark, the seagull calls,
People rest, street lights lit,
Bats in the belfry begin to flit
And the sun rises, the sun falls.

The town is still, there's nobody out,
Some will wake, if anyone shouts.
It's two hours till morning, then people will wake,
Instead of having a giant earthquake
And the sun rises, the sun falls.

The night is breaking and everyone is weak,
But children are ready to play hide-and-seek.
Tea is made, bacon is fried,
'Breakfast is made!' Mums cried
And the sun rises, the sun falls.

Thomas Heath (9)
Dodmire Junior School

The Sea

The sea, the sea
It's a wonderful thing
It comes in, it goes out
And its voice likes to sing

Its wave is like a hand
And it tickles the rocks
It goes in the caves
And washes up a box

The sea, the sea
Oh it's a wonderful thing
It comes in, it goes out
And its voice likes to sing.

Victoria Monk (7)
Dodmire Junior School

The Fantasy

Oceans blue with a blazing sun,
People with green hair and red skin
And sprinkles on top of a chocolate bun,
Gold and silver buildings with multicoloured glass.

Creatures with blue skin and yellow spots
And skies like an open sea,
With sweets and chocolate, lots and lots,
A bright yellow plane with camels and trees.

Cushions with red and white stripes
And chairs with a golden frame,
Gigantic houses with black and white pipes
And lime-green fields in the middle of a park.

David Lonsdale (11)
Dodmire Junior School

Football Crazy

Beckham's on the ball, he's going to score some goals
He goes to take a shot but there's Paul Scholes
Seaman's in the box saving all the shots
Jumping left, jumping right
Trying to get the ball out of sight
'We're going to score another goal,' says sweaty Andy Cole
Ronaldo getting nearer and nearer
Trying to get past Alan Shearer
You'll never guess who won?
Newcastle nil, Man U one!

Jordan Connelly (11)
Dodmire Junior School

The Football Poem

Football is fun,
Football is fine,
I love to play football all the time.

The roar of the fans,
The nerve of the game,
The players that score again and again.

The striker runs,
Down the left side,
Shoots but the ball goes wide.

The keeper stands,
So very tall,
Until he needs to save the ball.

Joshua Ward (8)
Dodmire Junior School

Mr Bean

What a jolly wally Mr Bean
He's even got his own magazine
But it is the funniest you've ever seen
He stuffed a turkey and stuck it on his head
Gasping for breath until he was nearly dead
On the other hand there is old, bossy Mrs Wicket
Everywhere she goes she is telling Bean where to stick it
And not to forget little teddy
Who travels all around the world, always ready
So there you have it
What a wally, Mr Bean.

Aarun Toor (11)
Dodmire Junior School

Let's Dance

Dance is like a free bird
At least that's what I've heard
Gracefully moving all night long
Jumping and singin' a song

So when you dance it is fun
Underneath the hot sun
Dance my friend, dance with thee
Because we can dance just you and me.

Rachel Chapman (8)
Dodmire Junior School

Coming To School

Feet pacing
 Children yelling
  School bags dragging
   Parents talking
    Cars leaving
     Infants crying
      Kids arriving
       Teachers breathing
        Hearts racing.

Mitchell Woodward (8)
Dodmire Junior School

Coming To School

Bags dragging
 Engines starting
  Cars arriving
   Dads driving
    Babies teething
     Teachers breathing
      Bell ringing
       Children singing.

Ashley Ruddam (9)
Dodmire Junior School

In The Park

Mums talking
 People walking
  Toddlers crying
  Birds flying
   Babies munching
    Squirrels crunching
    Leaves swooping
    Dogs looping
     Children going
     Water flowing
     Kids hiding
      Everyone's finding
      Girls singing
       Children swinging
       Aunties playing
       Uncles staying.

Rosie Elve (9)
Dodmire Junior School

Playing Football

Fans roaring
 Captains scoring
  Ref shouting
   Teams scouting
   Players yelling
   Others telling
   People going
    Whistle blowing
    Lights beaming
     Crowd screaming.

Charlotte Roscoe (8)
Dodmire Junior School

Football, Football

Football, football,
Kick the ball high.
Football, football,
Let it fly in the sky.

Football, football,
In the goal he scored.
Football, football,
How the crowd roared.

Football, football,
Pass it to a friend.
Football, football,
I don't want this to end.

Football, football,
Tension's getting high.
Football, football,
Gazza starts to cry.

Football, football,
Was it a tackle or a foul?
Football, football,
The crowd starts to growl.

Football, football,
1-0 the game did end.
Football, football,
What a great time I did spend.

Andrew Robinson (8)
Dodmire Junior School

Lucky, The Dog

Lucky, the dog is very crazy
But most of the time he's very lazy
Although in the morning he's up with the larks
And then he goes to play in the park
In the mud he rolls about
'Stop that!' I would shout
For I was the owner of this mad dog
Who rolled around in mud and a bog
In the house he'd get dried off
Whilst from the cold I would cough
When he was dry he'd chase the cat
And then when he was tired he'd flop on the mat
After, he'd chew on my shoes
Then he'd sit back down for another snooze
When he walks in the house he'll run
Then he'd go outside for a bit more fun
He'll chase me onto the road
And when he spots one, he chases a toad
After he goes in the park for a walk
He comes home to a dinner of pork
In between time he goes to sleep
So he curls up in a great big heap
I like to take Lucky everywhere with me
Because he's my friend and good company
I wish I could take him to my school
But he would get excited and act like a fool
We play together day and night
But we never ever have a fight
He likes to play with me and my friends
So mine and Lucky's friendship never ends.

Sarah Thompson (11)
Dodmire Junior School

The Wind Howls, The Wind Blows

The wind howls, the wind blows
The storm continues, the river flows
Trees creak, bend and snap
Thunder echoes with a clap
And the wind howls, the wind blows

The lightning strikes as trees fall
Owls give a mighty call
The storm makes floods as cars get stuck
And people fall in the sloppy muck
And the wind howls, the wind blows

The very next day
The storm went away
But some people say
It will be back the next day
And the wind howls, the wind blows.

Thomas Roscoe (8)
Dodmire Junior School

The Rain And The Lightning

As the rain bellows, then suddenly goes,
It leaves everything with drenched toes.
Flowers soaked, lawns puddle, soil to mud,
Has there ever been such a flood?
And the wind howls, the wind blows.

The lighting strikes and off it goes,
Leaving woods burned to the ground and burning,
Lightning flashes and gets louder,
Then rumbles down, it blazes everything,
Then it stops with a thundering clash.

John Wilson (8)
Dodmire Junior School

School

My school is really cool
We go swimming in the local pool
My teacher's name is Mrs Short
I hope she gives me a good report
The school meals are really nice
My favourite food is curry and rice

My school is really cool
The caretaker uses his tools
My favourite subject is art
I always take part
Whenever we do literacy
We always write a poem or three
When we go out to play
My friends shout 'Hooray'
My school is really cool.

Daisy Arrowsmith (8)
Dodmire Junior School

My Dog, Kia

Kia is a dog that never sleeps,
If she runs too fast she will land in a heap.

She never ever stops to eat,
But always steals the other dog's treat.

Because I don't like pancake,
I make a mistake and feed her a flake.

She does not like seeing the vet,
But all she does is get caught in the net.

Although she rips my pink coloured vests,
I've told you before, she is the best.

Melissa Holmes (8)
Dodmire Junior School

That's Me

There's me when I was one
It was my first time I had seen a swan

And there's me when I was two
I was hungry and I was licking my shoe

There's me when I was three
I was climbing an apple tree

And there's me when I was four
I was at the beach playing in the shore

There's me when I was five
I was in the pool trying to dive

And there's me when I was six
I was picking a pic 'n' mix

There's me when I was seven
I was on the train going to Devon

And there's me when I was eight
I was washing a plate

There's me when I was nine
I was pretty and so divine

Here I am and I am ten
And I don't want to start again.

Maria Jane Smith (8)
Dodmire Junior School

Batman

B eautiful sights at night with him
A mazing to see him fly
T raps evil empires trying to rule the world
M adman on run, Batman caught him and he's done
A mazing to see him free innocent people
N ightmares gone because of Batman.

Lewis Myers (9)
Dodmire Junior School

The Wind Howls, The Wind Blows

Everything in the driveway glows
Lightning flashing, putting on shows
The thunder is too loud, I can't hear
The only thing I feel is fear
And the wind howls, the wind blows

All the things I wanted to do
I'll have to stay in, as the clock goes cuckoo
The rain's still pouring, soaking wet
So I have to play with my train set
And the wind howls, the wind blows.

Daniel Toth (8)
Dodmire Junior School

My Baby Brother, Adam

The birth of my baby brother is the best gift I've ever had,
If I'm feeling lonely, he stops me feeling sad.
His cute smile warms up my heart,
For I cannot remember life without him from the start.
He has cute little fingers and cute little toes,
A cute little mouth and a sweet button nose.
He has soft brown hair and eyes of green,
For he is the cutest baby I have ever seen.
I am so glad he is my baby brother,
For I could not see him with any other.

Emma McAfee (10)
Dodmire Junior School

Playing Football

Crowd screaming
 Lights beaming
  Players scoring
   Managers roaring
    Scouts yelling
     Refs telling
      People going
       Whistle blowing
        Goalie jumping
         Teams thumping.

Jack Carson (9)
Dodmire Junior School

Outside

Babies crying
 Birds flying
  Dogs walking
   Mums talking
    Friends playing
     Chicken laying
      Dads looking
       Mums cooking
        Sisters meeting
         Brothers eating.

Lucy Earnshaw (9)
Dodmire Junior School

The Waterfall

Lively creature wild and free,
Astounding sight, high and tall,
Swishes and sways back and forth,
Sometimes calm, sometimes rapid,
All in all, an amazing sight.

Rachael Sturdy (9)
Dodmire Junior School

The Snow Queen

She's as fierce as a cheetah
As scary as a lion
So you better watch out!
Her blood is rose-red
And her hair is blizzard-white
So you better watch out!
She's an evil, nasty, rotten, clever
Icy-white *witch!*
She's very, very powerful
Her hands are like tinfoil
So you better watch out!
She has nails like a gerbil
And she's as thin as a chair leg
So you better watch out!
She's an evil, nasty, rotten, clever
Icy-white *witch!*

Arrianne Nelson (9)
Hartside Primary School

The Strange Table

At the silent, strange table
Alice made her way
She was greeted by the hatter
Who brightened up her day

Whilst the fluffy March hare
Stared into his tea
And was clearly thinking,
This doesn't seem like me

Alice looked at the dark tree
Where she saw the hatter sitting
Alice stared right at the hare
And thought, *won't he stop hitting?*

Rebecca Winter (9)
Hartside Primary School

The Lion

The lion, as dominating as a colonel,
Growling at its victim,
As violent as a cheetah on a food spree,
Feasting on its magnificent prey.

The lion, as furious as my dad,
So savage, he's the king of the jungle,
Breath as cold as the frostiest ice,
Staring, scanning for food.

Kurt Readman (9)
Hartside Primary School

My Dog, Jet

My four-legged animal lying around,
With his beautiful white face he runs around.
This beautiful black-furred mammal jumping happily.
My sharp-eyed species eating lunch,
This cute hairy animal sleeping peacefully.
My ravenous black-eyed savage animal searching swiftly.

Adrian Adamson (9)
Hartside Primary School

Details About Brown Bear

Dark brown bear eating the grass
Cute hairy mammal staring at me
Brown-eyed creature looking in the trees
Large-clawed species running around quickly
Strange-looking animal lying down quietly
This beautiful living thing nosing in the branches.

Laura George (10)
Hartside Primary School

Theseus' Challenge

When Theseus went into the maze
Ariadne says,
'Use this enchanted string
Good luck it will bring.'
Theseus was sly,
He made Ariadne cry.
When he left her on the rocks,
She was combing her locks.
Theseus is brave!
The crowd gave a wave
When Theseus came back
From the Minotaur's attack.
When King Aegeus saw the black sails,
He thought, *my son, he fails.*
He cried,
Then jumped into the sea and died!

Stacey Parkinson (8)
Hartside Primary School

Run, Run, It's The Minotaur

Run, run, it's the Minotaur!
He's coming to raid the town.
Run, run, it's the Minotaur!
He's stealing the king's bright crown.
Run, run, it's the Minotaur!
Theseus is being brave.
Run, run, it's the Minotaur!
Everyone's hiding in a cave.
Run, run, it's the Minotaur!
Theseus has grabbed a sword.
Run, run, no more,
The Minotaur is dead on the floor.

Megan Bryden (7)
Hartside Primary School

Theseus, My Son

'Son, Son, where are you going?
Son, Son, where are you going?
Son, Son, where are you going?
Tell me Son, where are you going?'

'I'm going to kill the Minotaur
I'm going to kill the Minotaur
I'm going to kill the Minotaur
That is where I'm going.'

'Take care my son
Take care my son
Take care my son
When you fight the Minotaur.'

'Show a white sail
Show a white sail
Show a white sail
On your safe return.'

Lauren Moore (8)
Hartside Primary School

The Minotaur

Meat, meat, he wants a lot of meat,
The Minotaur lives in Crete.

He's hairy
And scary.

He smells,
In a labyrinth he dwells.

He has massive jaws
And very sharp claws.

He's got hairy hands
And hairy, smelly feet.

Connor Thompson (8)
Hartside Primary School

Theseus

Theseus is brave,
He saved people's lives.

Theseus went to fight a monster
Called a Minotaur.

Theseus used magic thread
And used a dangerous sword.

Theseus became a king,
He wore a yellow crown.

Megan Scott (8)
Hartside Primary School

Labyrinth

In the middle of a labyrinth,
Enchanted string rolling on,
Through the labyrinth
Theseus walked,
Trailing the string behind,
Theseus find the Minotaur,
He kills it with a sword,
The ugly, terrible beast
Dead at last,
No more evil will he do.

Rebecca Pinder (8)
Hartside Primary School

The Minotaur

The Minotaur was mean,
Pointy horns,
Sharp teeth,
Half man, half beast,
Every seven years
Fourteen children he eats.

Katie Leigh (8)
Hartside Primary School

The White Rabbit Running Out Of Time

I'm late, I'm late, I'm totally late as my mate
I'm going to be late if I don't hurry up
My clock is late as my tea's getting made
I must hurry up to get there in time
I have to go fast, as fast as a motorbike
Or I will be late, as late as my mate
Again and again and every day's the same
I must hurry up or I will be so late
If I don't set my clock, I will be late every day.

Dominic Woloszyn (8)
Hartside Primary School

Snow White

Pretty young face looking hopeful
Black beautiful hair sparkling brightly
Wonderful cute eyes staring curiously
Little cold ears twitching slowly
Ragged ripped clothes hanging loosely
Small thin legs dancing happily
Sad soft arms moving dreadfully
Lovely long lips twinkling quietly.

Jamie-Lee Harding (9)
Hartside Primary School

The Flying Dragon

The flying dragon moves swiftly through the air
And his friend hops on his back
He sees the tidy towns go past
And sees children playing in playgrounds
The dragon has to fly down now
Because he's getting kind of sleepy
So shut your star-bright eyes
And enjoy your dream away.

Rachel Sewell (8)
Hartside Primary School

The Crooky Spooky Town Spell

The witch, the witch,
She's coming to town,
She's doing a spell,
So you better duck down.

The spell is loaded with fire frogs
And it's spookier than the four-headed dogs,
The dogs are strong, sly and cunning
And Snow White, well, she's just stunning.

The witch's spell, what she did,
Well, she's acting like a kid
And poor Snow White
What can we do?

The witch just might cast a spell on us too!

Emma Winter (9)
Hartside Primary School

The Witch

The witch, as vicious as an erupting volcano,
Her broom as fast as a full speed rocket,
Her disgusting face as green as goo
And her voice as croaky as a big, old toad.

The cat as furious as a raging bull,
His ball as huge as a giant,
His eyesight as clear as a crystal ball
And his friend as cheery as a chirping chaffinch.

So the witch and her cat, nasty as can be,
Both ran away into the violent sea.

Beth Moralee (9)
Hartside Primary School

The Dangerous Lion

The lion is more vicious than a giant
He is very petrifying
He is faster than a rocket
He is skinnier than a wrestler
He is smaller than a dog
He is sleepier than my grandma

The lion more dangerous than a dragon
The lion is more beautiful than a rainbow
He is smarter than my Uncle John
He is fatter than my sister
He has long and curly hair
He is big and terrifying
The lion is just the best.

Stefan Johnson (8)
Hartside Primary School

Balloo

Balloo, the pretty blue bear
Is as blue as the bluest day
Running through the sunlight
Having such a little fright

Balloo, a very amazing bear
He jumps, he drops, he plays
Yes, he's a very amazing bear
He sings, he laughs, he runs

Balloo is a very amazing bear.

Kaylee Pollitt (9)
Hartside Primary School

Spotted Owl

Brown spotted owl sleeping gracefully
This cuddly and cute species howling peacefully
Wide-eyed animal flying slowly
Feathered coloured bird perched silently
Furry, fluffy creature sleeping snugly
Good-tempered spotted owl focusing intelligently on its prey

The spotted owl.

Claire Hodkinson (10)
Hartside Primary School

The Minotaur

Long ago lived a terrible monster,
The Minotaur was its name,
Half man, half bull,
In a labyrinth it lived,
It had terrible teeth, sharp, long and pointed,
Bloodshot eyes and sharp, pointy horns.

Ellie Burns (8)
Hartside Primary School

Minotaur

A terrible monster
Half man, half beast
He is ugly
With sharp, pointed horns

He is evil
Disgusting
Eats humans
And all their juicy bits.

Bethany Howcroft (8)
Hartside Primary School

The Minotaur

Every seven years
To the Minotaur was sent
Seven girls and seven boys

The Minotaur will have a shock
For amongst the fourteen children
Is a young man, Theseus
The son of King Aegeus

With an enchanted ball of string
Theseus finds
And kills
The Minotaur.

Hannah Blakey (7)
Hartside Primary School

Ariadne

Ariadne, the daughter of an evil king,
Kind, helpful, loving,
Curly black hair,
Shiny white teeth,
Light brown eyes,
Bright red lips,
As pretty as a rose.

Natalie Hopper (8)
Hartside Primary School

Theseus

A brave young man
On his way to fight and kill
A terrifying monster
He saves Athens
His people too
A hero who is loved.

Scott Lavery (7)
Hartside Primary School

The Minotaur

The Minotaur is hungry
He wants some meat
He's evil
And likes human meat!
Half man, half beast
Sharp horns
With a hairy chest
Pointed teeth
Red, bloodshot eyes.

Evan Conley (7)
Hartside Primary School

The Minotaur

He wants some delicious meat
Half man and half bull
A very big monster
Horns like a knife
Some very bloody, horrible teeth
Lots of huge sharp claws
Two terrifying human ears
With very, very red eyes
The ugliest monster alive.

Ethan Campbell (8)
Hartside Primary School

The Minotaur

A mighty monster
Sharp, sharp teeth
Half man, half bull
Eyes like fire
Pointed horns
Blood between his teeth.

Samantha Sleights (8)
Hartside Primary School

The Minotaur

Terrifying monster
Wanting human meat
Half man, half beast
Gigantic horns
Hairy body
Sharp claws

Big head
Huge hooves
Always hungry
Wanting more.

Kalan Roberts (7)
Hartside Primary School

The Minotaur

Centuries ago
There was a Minotaur
He had snapping teeth
And the sharpest horns ever
Fireball eyes
A terrifying monster
Everyone he eats
Except Theseus
Whom he couldn't defeat.

Jacob Craig (7)
Hartside Primary School

Minotaur

A horrible monster who lives in the labyrinth
The Minotaur is an ugly beast
He has sharp horns, he is half human
And half animal.

Holly Howe (8)
Hartside Primary School

Mad Minotaur

The bad Minotaur has big feet,
He hates people, he eats meat,
He lives in a labyrinth,
It's in Crete,
He is nasty, cunning, sly,
He has a big red eye,
The Minotaur,
The Minotaur,
Run away from the Minotaur.

Meghan Nicholson (7)
Hartside Primary School

The Death Of The Minotaur

Theseus on to the Minotaur's back
He jumped
Stabbing him with a sword
Blood dripping everywhere
Sweat pouring down his face
Groans and moans
As the Minotaur dies.

Daniel Lawson (8)
Hartside Primary School

The Minotaur

Theseus was really frightened
Into the maze he went
Trailing string behind him
A terrible roar he hears
Theseus stops the Minotaur
Kills the Minotaur
With a flashing sword.

Georgina Parker (7)
Hartside Primary School

The Monkey

Active and quick monkey swinging gracefully through the trees,
Brown-faced species eating rapidly,
Exhausted and lousy animal lying wearily,
Prickly hairy mammal hanging tightly,
Jumping madly, creature fighting strongly,
Black-eyed living thing sleeping tediously.

The monkey.

Thomas Mason (10)
Hartside Primary School

Willow Tree

Old wrinkly willow tree drooping lifelessly,
Tall brown, no longer a living thing, died tragically,
Small pointy seed that grew so quickly,
Until thin and raggy,
Shabby spiny tree dead and ragged,
Bendy wispy plant limp in the wind,
The willow tree.

Holly Dixon (10)
Hartside Primary School

The Minotaur

The Minotaur, half man, half bull
Sharp teeth
Deadly horns
Red eyes
Hairy body
Loves delicious meat.

Ryan Scott (8)
Hartside Primary School

The Bengal Tiger

The furry and cuddly Bengal tiger
Pounces swiftly at its enemies
This sharp-clawed species licks its body slowly
Carnivorous animal devours its prey ravenously
Brown-eyed creature staring over the canopy
Orangey-black mammal caring for its babies

The Bengal tiger.

Anthony Gale (9)
Hartside Primary School

The Jet-Black Puma

Jet-black puma dashing through the trees,
Very fast mammal hunting its prey.
Yellow-eyed animal devouring messily,
Rough ferocious species drinking.
Vicious beastly wildlife prowling around,
Sharp-toothed carnivore sprinting barbarically.

The jet-black puma.

Holly Craig (10)
Hartside Primary School

The Hamster

This cute cuddly hamster scurries quickly on his running wheel,
Sharp-clawed fur-ball climbing his cage swiftly,
Red-eyed mammal nibbles happily on his food,
Brown furry animal runs energetically in its cage,
This small tiny creature carries his food mouthfully,
Brown and white-headed species staring sharply at a cat.

Callum Futter (9)
Hartside Primary School

The White Tiger

Great white tiger searching sharply
Black-eyed mammal sleeping peacefully
Short-tempered species pouncing on its prey
White and black animal sitting patiently on a root of a large tree
Sharp-clawed creature eating carnivorously
The black and white tiger defending its habitat
The white tiger.

Shelby Timoney (9)
Hartside Primary School

Red Panda

This light brown mammal hunts for food
Red panda species clinging on the brown branch
A wonderful rare creature finding juicy red berries
Dark brown-eyed animal clawing on the tree top
Large, quick panda running around fast
Furry, adorable red panda scurrying across the grass
Red panda.

Lauren Hutchinson (10)
Hartside Primary School

The Monkey

Cute furry monkey swinging energetically through the bushy trees
Cuddly soft mammal feeding on delicious bananas fresh
                                        from the rainforest
Kind natured animal, is loving and caring
Brown cheeky species sweetly cuddling its tiny baby

The monkey.

Beth Dawson (9)
Hartside Primary School

The Hamster

Furry warm hamster sniffing strongly
Itchy small species scratching sharply
Starving hungry creature eating quickly
Sharp-toothed species gnawing on the bars of the cage
Black-eyed dark-coloured rodent looking sharply for food
Tired cosy fur-ball sleeping in its bed

The hamster.

Matthew Allan (10)
Hartside Primary School

A Bird Called Pepsie

This grey and black creature dancing peacefully in her cage
Small-eyed animal whistling beautifully all night long
This lovely fluffy thing sleeping quietly in its home
This cute and feathered species dancing and swinging on its swing
The sharp-beaked bird pecking and sharpening her claws
The bird called Pepsie.

Kayleigh Abbott (10)
Hartside Primary School

The Sloth

This three-toed sloth lying upside down
The dark-eyed mammal swaying peacefully
This beautiful creature clinging gracefully
The dark brown bodied animal sleeping quietly
The white-faced species gazing into space

The sloth.

Stephanie Parker (9)
Hartside Primary School

Smokey

Pitch-black dog squeaking happily,
Warm furry mammal sleeping peacefully,
Cute cuddly species awaking wearily,
Old bearded creature lying lazily,
This beautifully trained male staring constantly.

Alex Hall (10)
Hartside Primary School

My Two Best Friends

I have two best friends called Lucy and Laura,
Lucy tells me secrets that even her family does not know,
We've all known each other all our . . . *life!*
Laura and me sit together in class,
We've never moved away,
Me and Laura share everything,
I've known her since I was two or three,
I sometimes fall out with them,
But we make up
And both are very special!

Anya Campbell (9)
Hunwick Primary School

Friendship Poem

Friendship
Is fun,
Magical,
Happy,
You're never left out,
Never give up on a friend,
Because
Friendship lasts forever.

Lucy Hedley (8)
Hunwick Primary School

Bullies

When I got bullied I said to myself
'Why do they need to do that?'
The next day they came along
And threw snowballs at me
It made me feel sad
They think that they are hard
But they aren't
They are soft
They are jealous of others
They do it because they got bullied themselves.

Jasmine Graham (8)
Hunwick Primary School

Bullies

Bullies think they're so smart,
Why do bullies pick on you?
Bullies make fun of you,
Bullies are so, so awful,
Awful bullies whisper behind your back
And call you names,
Big bullies think they're strong,
Bullies are jealous because
They're not very happy.

Wallis Greaves (8)
Hunwick Primary School

Friends

Friends are kind all the time.
Friends are helpful when I am stuck.
Friends play with you in the yard.
Friends are funny.
Friends share with you.
Friends are there for you.

Rebecca Hawthorne (9)
Hunwick Primary School

Friendship Poem

Were your friends always there for you to be a friend?
Mine was . . .
Was there a person to tell your secrets to
Or help you to do things?
Mine was. . . .
Were your friends there if you were sad?
Mine was . . .
Was your friend a best friend?
Mine was
Did your friend keep your secrets?
Mine did!

Josh Keig (9)
Hunwick Primary School

Bullies

Bullies are cowards,
They bully you at school,
They make fun of you,
Bullies call you names,
They talk behind your back,
They hassle you,
Bullies are bad and mean,
They gang up on you.

Daniel Bennett (8)
Hunwick Primary School

Bullies

Bullies think they are smart.
Bullies think they are tall.
Bullies think they are awful.
Bullies think they are great.
Bullies think they are strong,
But it's mostly the big ones.

Stephanie Bennett (8)
Hunwick Primary School

Bullies

Bullies sometimes run away when you try to catch up
Bullies are nasty to you when you are nice to them
Bullies shout at you and call you names
Bullies look at you and walk away
Bullies sometimes hit you and pick on you
Bullies talk about you behind your back
Bullies think they are harder and wiser than you
Bullies bully you mostly at school and home
Bullies hassle you in the classroom
Bullies are really cowards!

Biancha Tarran (10)
Hunwick Primary School

Sally And Anya

I have two best friends,
They've told me secrets,
Anya invited me to sleep,
Sally invited me over too,
My friends are the best and special,
Anya and Sally have known me since I was three!
I sit next to Anya in class,
We share the laptops,
We'll be best friends forever.

Laura Bradshaw (8)
Hunwick Primary School

Friends

Friends are caring when you're sad,
Friends are kind because they play with you,
Friends are always nice to you,
Friends share sweets with you,
Friends teach you lessons.

Callum Hodgson (9)
Hunwick Primary School

My Grandma Is A Witch!

My grandma is a witch,
Well, that's what I think,
She reads in the most strangest ways,
She plays cricket on a football pitch!

My grandma is a witch,
Well, that's what I think,
On a night when she's watching Neighbours,
My grandad is doing her big favours,
I can hear her cackle and laugh,
I've seen her huge big staff!

My grandma is a witch,
Well, that's what I think,
Don't worry, I've thought it all out,
When we were on the M62
She needed the loo,
So I locked her in there forever!

Sally Pentecost (8)
Hunwick Primary School

Friendship Poem

Did you friend forget
About your birthday
Or eat your sweets
Or pinch your bike?
Mine did

Did your friend
Break up with you
And never make up
And be horrible?
Mine did

Did your friend ever
Make up or be nice?
Mine didn't.

Lauren Hawthorne (9)
Hunwick Primary School

My Friendship Poem

Was your friend always there for you when you were by yourself?
Mine was.

Was your friend kind to you when you were feeling sad?
Mine was.

Was your friend your best friend?
Mine was.

Did your friend trust you?
Mine did.

Is your friend called Chelsea?
Mine is.

Nicole Green (9)
Hunwick Primary School

My Best Friend

Was your friend there when your friends left you?
Mine was.

Was your friend there when you were upset?
Mine was.

Do you trust your friend?
I do.

Did your friend make you upset?
Mine did.

Megan Maddison (8)
Hunwick Primary School

My Best Friend

Does your friend
Pull faces at you,
Talk behind your back
And be nasty to you?

Mine did.

Does your friend
Shout at you,
Give your secrets away
And tell of you?

Mine did.

Does your friend
Play with you,
Keep your secrets
And be kind?

Mine does.

Chloe Green (9)
Hunwick Primary School

Bullies

Bullies bully everyone
Because they're sad.
Bullies bully everyone
Because they're bored.
Bullies bully everyone
Because they're selfish.
Bullies bully everyone
Because they can't win.

Jamie Campbell (9)
Hunwick Primary School

Babies Are So . . .

Babies are so tidy,
Babies are so neat,
But there's only one problem,
They eat things they shouldn't eat.

Babies are so bald,
Babies like to kick,
Babies always cry,
But babies are so thick.

Alex Bradshaw (8)
Hunwick Primary School

Friends

My friends tell me secrets
And I tell them mine.
I know that her favourite sweets are liquorice,
She shares her sweets with me,
We share our clothes sometimes,
Her favourite colours are blue and pink.

Ellie Pryce (9)
Hunwick Primary School

Popcorn

The corn leaps in and around, hard and cold,
The machine begins to whirr and rattle,
Smell the fumes as the corn explodes,
Shooting out, stopping it will be a battle,
Out it comes in a different shape,
Like people rushing out of a fire escape,
Tasty and sweet,
Lots to eat!

Freddie Metcalfe (9)
Ingleton CE Primary School

Fireworks

Sudden floods of colour
In the sky
Shimmering once or twice
Upon each leering eye

The dusty sparks fall to the ground
Catherine wheels float like halos
Crowning each rocket's beauty
Eternalising each miracle

Similar to an orchestra
Rising in a crescendo
An exodus to the sky
Reaching their final destination

Stars so jealous of each
Flourishing delicate flower
Painted by an artist; better than
Picasso, dies to a fizzle.

Jon Ainsley (11)
Ingleton CE Primary School

Fireworks

F laming fireworks escape from the rocket
I n an attempt to cascade the land
R eturning to the ground
E very colour in the land
W hirling in the midnight sky
O ver the world it collapses
R ound and round, down to the ground
K aleidoscopic to the ground
S uddenly they have gone.

Bethany Payne (9)
Ingleton CE Primary School

Waterfall

Crashing past the sandy bed,
Swifting over the red salmon's head,
Flying out to the world below,
Over the end and off we go.

Hitting the bottom with a fragile boom,
Silently singing under the midnight moon,
Gobbling and swallowing the little scuttling fish,
Lit up with the sunset, such a beautiful wish.

Hilly Redgrave (11)
Ingleton CE Primary School

Popcorn

It's like a rosebud popping into a rose,
It pops out like a spurting hose,
It pops out like a bouncy ball,
Hitting us all,
We eat it with a crunch,
We munch and we munch,
We put butter on it,
It makes it taste terrific.

Annabel Franks (9)
Ingleton CE Primary School

Popcorn

Grains tumbling, suspense growing,
Excitement gathering, faces glowing,
Suddenly *pop! bang!* all around,
Hear the wonderful popping sound,
Have a sniff, have a smell,
Popcorn exploding from its shell.

Sam Hunter (9)
Ingleton CE Primary School

Fireworks

Fireworks erupting around me everywhere,
I come to a halt and stare,
Like the spiral swishing around,
I turn and face the night-time sky,
Colours smother the valley in emerald and ruby-white,
Then the colours dwindle away into the night.

Kayleigh Toms (10)
Ingleton CE Primary School

Popcorn

Rattles in the volcano, heating up and popping
Up goes the popcorn flying and dropping
Volcano gets hotter, cooking more popcorn
Just waiting to be popped
It popped all over your lawn.

Daniel Westgarth (10)
Ingleton CE Primary School

Fireworks

First of all you are standing waiting
Then you see a torpedo firing
With a *bang* the torpedo's gone
But now you see where the colours are from.

Alexander Clark (10)
Ingleton CE Primary School

The Blitz

Whirring warns of the doodlebug's advance
Silence, has it gone? Is there a chance?
The siren screams, the children cry,
Mothers shield them as walls tumble, why?

Samuel Forster (10)
Ingleton CE Primary School

Fireworks

F ireworks burst
I n colourful showers of
R uby, crimson and
E merald like apples
W aiting
O verhead
R ockets burst and bang like
K ings of the sky.

Oliver Armstrong (9)
Ingleton CE Primary School

Autumn Leaves

When all around the wind doth blow,
The moon stars glitter and glow,
Squirrels scurrying in the crisp leaves,
Leaves flutter down the swaying trees,
Leaves cascading down the bark,
Falling and falling until it's dark,
The trees are bowing before me
And at the end, I see no more trees.

Charlotte Marshall (11)
Ingleton CE Primary School

Popcorn

The popcorn's popping
Then it's stopping
Then it's smelling
And the children are yelling
Then it's jumping
Cracking, something.

Peter K Armstrong (10)
Ingleton CE Primary School

Transplant

T ransforming my life
R eaping
A way my soul
N earing my
S olution
P utting my
L ife at risk
A nd saving another
N early there
T hen I'm gone!

Adam Bourne (10)
Ingleton CE Primary School

Autumn Leaves

A utumn leaves like
U shers welcoming people
T he leaves are like feathers fluttering to the ground
U selessly sitting watching
M urmuring to them as they
N atter back.

Rebecca Parker (10)
Ingleton CE Primary School

Snow

Let the stillness grow,
When there is a world full of snow.
It covers the world in its white veil,
Is it whiter than the winter's mail?

Samantha Weatherburn (11)
Ingleton CE Primary School

New Pet

I've got a new pet
But I don't know what to call it
I keep thinking of the most ridiculous names
But they don't seem right

I've just thought
I need to get some hay for it
And straw
Plus loads of other things

I need a brush
Lots of food
A water bowl
What am I going to do?

Where am I going to keep it?
In the garden
In the garage
It'll need lots of exercise
I'll have to take it out daily!

What will the neighbours think?
I hope they don't get mad
Though that little old lady across the road
Won't be happy if it makes the smallest noise

I've got used to Sid now
Though he can be a bit of a handful
I never realised having an elephant as a pet could be this hard!

Emma Sisk (9)
Mowden Junior School

A Ghoulish Couple

Ghoulie girl said to ghoulie boy . . .
'You're full of fleas
You stink of old green cheese!
I love your purple warts
And you absolutely hate sports
I admire your horrible, filthy ways
And your bloodshot gaze'

Ghoulie boy said to ghoulie girl . . .

'I love your pointy nose
Your black and grey clothes
Your teeth are yellow
And you're a fat kind of fellow!
Your hairy knees
I think you are smaller than trees
You only have one shoe
But I will still love you.'

Nicola Dennis (10)
Mowden Junior School

Down At The Bottom Of The Ocean!

Down at the bottom of the ocean,
Where I saw a fish,
I saw a submarine,
A shark or two,
I even saw a kangaroo,
Boing, boing, boing,
Down at the bottom of the ocean,
I saw a scuba-diver,
Coral I saw,
Don't touch it or you will get a prick,
Owwww!

Connie Archer (7)
Mowden Junior School

Cats

Furry cat
Fat cat
Skinny cat
Nasty cat
Tall cat
Small cat
City cat
Farm cat
Ugly cat
Pretty cat
House cat
Wild cat
Noisy cat
Quiet cat
Clumsy cat
Wise cat
Too many cats!

Ian Wilson (9)
Mowden Junior School

Forest Song

Dark, damp, draughty, lurking
The forest is asleep

Leafy, light, green, shadowy
The forest is awakening

Streams, creatures, birds, beasts
The forest is alive

Silent, cold, frosty
The forest is tired!

Sarah Grainger (10)
Mowden Junior School

The Royal Wedding

Here comes the queen in robes of emerald-green,
Followed by the king carrying a glittering ring,
Here comes the prince who wished he could hide,
Following behind comes the blushing bride.

The bride's parents were all a-fluster,
As the crowds stood all in a cluster
And the bridesmaids went round with a duster.

The minister looked sinister,
The groom looked doomed,
The bride looked flushed.

As they said their vows,
There was an expectant wow,
The bride smiled saying, 'I do' while blushing too.

The groom looked proud as he looked round,
They kissed and the crowd made no sound,
The crowd sat down.

The groom and bride smiled,
As they departed down the aisle,
While the choir left in single file.

The bells rang as everyone sang,
Husband and wife departed,
Trusting they would never be parted.

Jennifer English (8)
Mowden Junior School

My Brother's Stinky Socks

My brother's socks stink
He's got blue ones, green and even pink!
He hangs them up around the house
The smell's strong enough to kill the mouse!

He makes booby traps in my room
And when I walk in . . . *boom!*
They always fall on top of my head
And then I trip onto my bed!

Now Mum and I got sick of this
So Mum sat down and gave him a kiss
She said, 'Stop being horrible to your sister'
My brother said 'Sorry' and then he kissed her

But he still didn't stop playing tricks
And his attitude, we told him to fix
But that's just how my brother is
And with a mum like mine, I'm surprised he still lives!

Jessica Burton (9)
Mowden Junior School

What Is Yellow?

Yellow is the sunshine blazing with all its might,
Yellow is a light bulb shining nice and bright,
Yellow is my ball I bounce upon the ground,
Yellow is my stunt kite flying all around.

Yellow is some flowers growing in a pot,
Yellow is a kettle boiling very hot,
Yellow is a car driving down the street,
Yellow is the socks I wear upon my feet.

Yellow is the ribbon in my long brown hair,
Yellow is the autumn leaves dancing through the air,
Yellow is the colour of my Winnie the Pooh,
That's what I think is yellow, do you?

Stephanie Wilson (7)
Mowden Junior School

Why Oh Why Does It Rain?

Why, oh why does it rain?
I guess the trees are in pain
The swollen clouds
Burst out aloud
And that's why I think it rains

Why, oh why does it rain?
The earth is thirsty, dry and drained
Some food we eat
Comes from beneath
And that's why I think it rains

Why, oh why does it rain?
The children love to play again and again
Out in the puddles
They all hug and cuddles
And that's why I think it rains

Now I know why it rains
Man and plants depend on its gains
So when I see the sky all black and mean
I will smile because I know it is not a dream.

Danielle Murdock (8)
Mowden Junior School

There Was Once A Boy Called Sam

There was once a boy called Sam,
Who really gobbled up ham.
One day none was there,
It was a big scare,
So instead he ate up some jam.

Sam Shield (8)
Mowden Junior School

Football Poem

Players running across the pitch,
Feeling extra good.
One or two tumble over
And get all covered in mud.

The ball is very smooth
And its shape very round.
It is kicked all over the pitch,
In air and on the ground.

The cup is very safe,
Sitting on a seat.
A single player can win it,
Using both his feet.

The game comes to an end,
The crowd all stand and cheer.
One team won with a single goal,
The other was very near.

Connor Shield (8)
Mowden Junior School

Winter's Over

Winter's over,
No more snow,
The flowers coming up to grow,
Leaves are green,
Winter's been,
Green grass dreams,
As the sunshine gleams,
Sunflowers tall,
Spiders crawl
And I can dream,
That winter's been.

Lauren McQuaker (11)
Mowden Junior School

Snail

The slimy snail slithers slowly,
Crossing cavernous cans,
The shed is dark, damp, dangerous place,
For a snail.

Lots of lovely lettuces;
He has left the shed
And is in the great green garden;
But poisonous pellets are dangerous
For a snail.

A giant green stem,
Mountains of mud;
He is in an oval orange object, a flowerpot;
But a big blue bird comes; very dangerous
For a snail.

A lovely large leaf,
Secure safety,
A shelter from sieges
For a snail!

Calum Williams (10)
Mowden Junior School

Fish

Fish swimming in the sea
Splosh, splosh, splosh
They definitely get a great
Wash, wash, wash

Swish, swish
Go their fins
Flip-flop go their tails
Fish swimming everywhere!

Isabel Walker (7)
Mowden Junior School

The Sea

The sea splashes,
Crashes and swirls,
Spraying the cliffs,
Eating up the sand and rocks,
Dipping and dropping,
Stranding people,
Soaking people,
Wrecking sandcastles,
Giving ships a hard time,
Creating caves and tunnels,
Bashing against the rocks,
Destroying houses,
Washing the beach.

Home to sea life,
Coral reefs in shallow water,
Deep blue world ready to be explored.

Matthew Hewitson (10)
Mowden Junior School

A Quick Nip

A quick nip,
A little slip,

Little claws,
Cute, fluffy paws,

Beady eyes,
Chases flies,

Soothing purr,
Comforting fur,

Long, furry tail,
Nose small and pale,

Despises a rat,
Of course I'm a cat.

Liam Innis (9)
Mowden Junior School

Spring Vs Summer

Spring to serve,
Summer returns,
Wind gets a nasty blow,
One set a piece now,
Flower to serve,
With that blooming smile,
Hit hard across court,
An ace by flower,
Sun to serve,
Sun does his
Super stinger serve,
Another ace!
Great tennis a the seasons open,
Match point,
Wind gives a blowing serve,
Sun returns,
A slam by wind,
Flowers shoots,
Sun and flower win!
Summer is here.

Joshua Egglestone (10)
Mowden Junior School

Feelings

Am I happy?
Am I sad?
Am I feeling bad?

Am I angry?
Am I annoyed?
Am I feeling a bit destroyed?

Am I distraught?
Am I a bit caught?
Do I have to be taught?

Jonathan Morgan (10)
Mowden Junior School

My Dog

My dog is vicious and quite scary,
He's really mad and quite hairy,
He barks at cats and windows too
And he also tries to bite you.

He chops posts with teeth of steal
And he makes cats his meal,
He bites the door and grabs the post,
To other dogs he will just boast.

He is very angry every day
And always gets his barking say,
So when the vet sits on his seat,
He pulls back in retreat.

Shaun Bradley (10)
Mowden Junior School

Who Is It?

It flies high
Higher than trees
Always higher
Never lower
He beats his wings
A great force blown away
People get blown away
Silent groans
All not known
Unlucky creature
Gets taken away
To its doom
Fairy tale or not?
It's a dragon.

Jordan Lauder (11)
Mowden Junior School

Life

The start was then
And by then I knew
That I would have to live
A whole life through

I was four years old
And they promised they
Would let me go to school
The very next day

College was good
And college was great
But I had to stay
Until I was 28

I thought about jobs
Carefully
I decided on a tax officer
Collecting fees

When I got old
And I went to a home
I didn't make any friends there
So I was all alone

One day God
Decided to suspend
The journey
That has now come to an end.

Michael Hahn (10)
Mowden Junior School

The World Is Great

It's a big wide world out there,
There's no need for anyone to get scared
And this is how to make the world a bit better,
No more gamblers or the odd better.

The world is fantastic,
A great place to live in,
But we could make the world a better place,
By getting rid of all the disgrace.

If you knew what was happening,
In other places, not here,
If you help people in your neighbourhood,
The world will be more exciting than good.

If you see someone getting bullied,
Tell someone, quick, now hurry,
Europe, Africa and Asia too,
Will the world make peace? It's up to you.

If you love the world then you'll love life,
If you don't, then you'll just have to ride,
The world is fun if you just get to know it,
The problem is, some people don't show it.

David Wilson (11)
Mowden Junior School

The Net

Surfing the net can be so much fun
An e-mail account of your very own
Talking to friends and passing jokes
Playing games with other folks
It's not always safe and there are lots of dangers!
You need to be careful and not talk to strangers!

Liam Lynch (8)
Mowden Junior School

The Seasons Monster

Spring is the time when the monster unleashes,
Who walks about casually but rips you to pieces,
So beware in spring when the monster will strike
And especially beware if you're out on a hike.

Summer is the time which he tries to be cunning,
He hides in the bushes and sends people running,
Summer is when he's incredibly mad
And if you escape he'll turn totally sad.

Autumn is where he starts to sleep,
Who comes out occasionally, you might get a peep,
Then eventually he will lie back straight
And he'll wake back in the winter . . . late.

Do not wake him or you'll be sad,
Well, I would too if he were mad,
So leave him be till he wakes,
'Cause he'll be crying for goodness sake.

Matthew Rowan (10)
Mowden Junior School

Tiger

He stands there staring at his prey,
The sun gleaming down where he lay,
Fast asleep he falls,
But the birds are wide-awake shouting their calls,
As quiet as can be, he waits for footsteps of a goat,
He does not like to hurt his furry coat,
Now he has caught his bird,
But a cat is walking by, she purrs,
The tiger is too tired to chase,
Night falls, he hides behind a bush, just in case . . .

Leanne Jones (11)
Mowden Junior School

Rock Chick Grandma

My grandma is a rock chick
She wears designer clothes
She likes to have a drink
And looks trendy wherever she goes

She wears Gucci perfume
And has lots of shoes and clothes
Handbags are her fetish
And she looks younger than her years

Her hobby is doll houses
She decorates them all around
It costs her a small fortune
But she spends all the pounds

She has lots of friends
And she knows everyone around
You'll find her at the beach in summer
Getting a tan on the sand

On Mondays she babysits
On Tuesdays she's down the town
On Wednesday she works hard
And on Thursdays she lazes around

My grandma is a superstar
She makes sure everyone's OK
She spoils me rotten
I think she deserves to be in this poem today.

Brooklyn Armstrong (9)
Mowden Junior School

Snow Is Like . . .

Snow is like sugar
All over the tops of houses

Snow is like confetti
Sprinkled all over the world

Snow is like feathers
Softly falling to the ground

Snow is like tissues
Soft and gentle

Snow is like a white blanket
All over the world

Snow is like ripped up pieces of paper
Being walked in

Snow is like crystals
Glittering on the ground

Snow is like paint
Being painted all over the world

Snow is like clouds
Coming down from Heaven

Snow is like a white puffy polar bear
Lying on the ground

Snow is like cotton wool
Coming down from the sky

Snow is like frozen rain
Getting softer as it gets near the ground

Snow is like little diamonds
Falling to the ground

Snow is like . . .

Zohrah Malik (9)
Mowden Junior School

The River

Splash!
Out of the spring
And down the stream he flows,
Gurgling on the way,
Doesn't know where he's going,
Hitting rocks, even more
Confused.

Suddenly he knows,
So, gradually getting
Faster and faster,
He's off,
Rushing and speeding,
Crashing into rocks
And over the waterfall.

Whoosh! Into the river,
Crushing rocks,
Sometimes getting
Overcrowded.

Nearing the sea,
The journey shall end,
Finally he's there,
The sea splashing angrily,
But the river's not giving up,
Here's one last
Splash!

Nicholas Gordon (11)
Mowden Junior School

Tiger

Hunting for food,
Hunting, hunting.

Sneaking swiftly,
Sneaking, sneaking.

Like dart to board,
Darting, darting.

Disguised in the undergrowth,
Disguised, disguised.

Eyes searching,
Searching, searching.

Looking for prey,
Looking, looking.

Hiding in grass,
Hiding, hiding.

Moving stealthily,
Stealthily, stealthily.

Hungrily waiting,
Waiting, waiting.

Gazelles grazing,
Grazing, grazing.

Not expecting,
Expecting, expecting.

A blur of stripes,
Stripes, stripes.

Sprinting towards the herd,
Scattering, scattering.

Pouncing on a helpless animal,
Pouncing, pouncing.

Eaten!

Iona Hill (10)
Mowden Junior School

Fish

Fish,
Swims slowly around without a care,
Mouth open wide,
Two beady eyes stare,
An old man stumbling,
Now a graceful dancer,
Swishing and swaying,
Gurgling and gargling.

Fish's bigger brother,
Snaps a pair of pearly teeth,
Glides swiftly through the deep sea,
Crouches, ready to pounce,
Ready to kill,
It shoots up and grabs fish.

Shark rests peacefully,
Fish rests in peace.

Emily Kent (10)
Mowden Junior School

Wind

Wind swishing, swaying,
Rattling at the window,
Crashing at the door,
Dancing through the leaves,
Hiding in the bushes,
As strong as a bull,
As timid as a mouse,
Flying up and down,
Heard but never seen,
It's everywhere,
But never gone,
That mighty wind.

Gregory Boulby (11)
Mowden Junior School

Life In The Playground

Children running around
On the hard asphalt ground
Some playing tig
Or just walking

I like to play football
But I'm not very good
People like to play-fight
But afterwards they might hit

Footballs hitting faces
Without any care
People pushing and shoving
And pulling people's hair

Children falling over
And grazing their knee
Teachers sorting out things
And wasting their time

Children playing games
And walking in the mud
Suddenly the bell rings
And everyone lines up
So that is playtime.

Jonathan Coates (9)
Mowden Junior School

Fishes

Fishes swimming in the harbour,
All the fishes swim together,
In the rain and other weather,
They can swim, they're so clever,
Fishes swimming in the sea,
Types of fishes for you and me,
Some are camouflaged that you can't see,
In swimming they must have a degree!

David Freary (10)
Mowden Junior School

I Left My Body

I left my legs in bed
And then walked down the street.
I lost my arm on the farm
And still write very neat.

My head fell off and then I saw
That it was rolling down the hill.
I left my brain in my house,
On the window sill.

My ribs fell out,
I gave a shout.
How am I to survive?
If I keep losing my body, I will not be alive.

I found my legs in my bed
And also found my arm.
It was so strange because I thought
I'd left it on the farm.

I found my ribs in a garden,
They were on a BBQ,
I got them back
And said, 'Thank you.'

My head I found
Down a drain,
So I picked it up
And put it on again.

I then searched for my brain,
I found it in the sink,
I opened my head and popped it in
And now I can think.

I've got my body front,
So I jumped down with joy
And despite a little blood,
I'm still a normal boy.

Adam Craig (10)
Mowden Junior School

The Labyrinth

And so our story starts
And a young man departs
It was a dark and dangerous night
Ahead was a courageous fight

All his senses alert
Treading footprints in the dirt
He enters the cave of mystery
Even with his torch it's hard to see

Corridor after corridor, dead ends
The labyrinth never ends
He went through tunnels of fire
By now he began to tire

He curled up in a heap
And drifted off to sleep
Next day he found a chamber of gold
And in the burning centre behold

A fiery-red dragon held a dead knight
For the young man it was a terrible sight
He drew his sword of silver to fight
And the roar of the dragon ripped through the night

The sword struck on shiny scales
And screams of terror mixed with wails
Finally the dragon fell to the ground
In its own blood it was drowned

The man took as much gold as he could
He left the cave and went through the wood
At the castle he gave the gold to the poor
They'll never be hungry or sad anymore

Later that day, the cathedral bells ring
As the bishop crowns the brave new *king!*

Robert Smith (9)
Mowden Junior School

My Green Leaf

My green leaf is as green as can be,
As green as moss or when I'm ill as green as me.
My green leaf is as green as ever,
When it will die, I don't know but it may be never.

The massive sun is extremely hot,
Though very hot it's never been in a pot.
The massive big sun is never blue,
But when he is smiling, Mr Watkinson is too!

The beautiful red rose
Is always doing a pose.
The thorns on her stalk,
Make it so she cannot walk.

Snow is falling from the sky,
When I was five I thought it could fly.
Soft, white snow lying on the ground,
When I dance in it, I go round and round.

Beth Tulloch (8)
Mowden Junior School

Life In The Playground

Waiting for the bell to ring
Off it goes
Everyone out to play
Boys playing football
Girls playing netball
Children running, tripping over
Footballs flying through the air
Children playing tig
One boy falls over
A nasty graze
Blood dripping from his knee
Hide-and-seek, can you find me?
The bell rings
Off we go into line.

Ryan Blewitt (10)
Mowden Junior School

Rose Fairy

Lovely pink, red that glows
Or its lovely pearl-white
Are the colours of the rose.
The rose that's such a wonderful delight,
Such a lovely sweet smell,
The buds open then close,
Just as if it's a ringing bell,
How great it is to be fairy of the rose.

Catherine Parnaby (9)
Mowden Junior School

Wolves

Cunning, dark green eyes,
Power of a super car,
Tail like a sword,
Sleek black coat,
Powerful paws too big for itself,
Deep black nose like a radar,
Teeth sharp as knives,
Selfish claws glinting,
Hunting all night.

James Philip (10)
Mowden Junior School

The Magic Wellington

There was a man from Darlington,
He had a magic Wellington,
He wished to go to Washington,
But he ended up in Edmonton,
He wished to go back to Darlington,
But he lost his Wellington,
So he was stuck in Edmonton,
That is the *Endmonton*.

David Woodward (10)
Mowden Junior School

I'm Bursting For The Toilet, Miss

I'm bursting for the toilet, Miss
I really have to tell
I'm bursting for the toilet, Miss
I think I heard the bell
I'm bursting for the toilet, Miss
I think my bottom's getting sore
I'm bursting for the toilet, Miss
I can't wait anymore
I'm bursting for the toilet, Miss
I really have to go
I'm bursting for the toilet, Miss
I don't think I could wait an hour, no, no, no!

Look Miss, I really have to go!

Nicole Pinder (10)
Mowden Junior School

Flipper

Splish-splosh
Flip-flop
The dolphin is here riding the waves,
Swishing his tail like a feather fan.
Sun beating down on his shiny back,
Casting a ray of light to cover the ocean.
Jumping up in all his glory,
Flipper dives back to the dark world below,
Gliding through as smooth as a snake,
Dodging round rocks and weeds,
Into the cave of a king,
Where the darkness is darker than dark.
Still, silent - he's gone.

Emma Bartram (10)
Mowden Junior School

Money

Gimme gold, gimme silver, gimme diamonds and jewels,
Gimme mansions, gimme fame and big swimming pools,
The gold is shiny, the diamonds are good,
I got my money as fast as I could,
I robbed a bank, I robbed some shops,
Out came the police, known as the cops.

I flew away to a faraway land,
Diamond intact and money in hand,
They kept on following, I don't know why!
The CIA and the FBI,
The world was after me,
That's how I felt,
I was being a coward,
I felt like a whelp.

But I still had my money,
That's all that matters,
I stared at the sapphires,
Like a mad hatter,
There's still something there, which is like trickling honey,
If there's anything that was good, it was all that money.

Jared Kelvey-Brown (11)
Mowden Junior School

Birthday!

B is for birthday, what this poem is about,
I is for icing, which is on my cake,
R is for Rudolph, oops! Wrong time of year . . .
T is for tear, which I do to the wrapping paper,
H is for hearth, which is what I sit by while I open my presents,
D is for dog which I got for my birthday,
A is for amplifier, which I need for my guitar,
Y is for years old, which changes every *birthday!*

Nicholas Bruce (11)
Mowden Junior School

The Deep, Dark Forest

She sways angrily in the bitter storm,
Spellbound in the witch's charm,
The forest trickles over like waves crashing on the shore,
Crawling with wildlife at her feet,
Whistles . . . whistles in the deep,
The chill of the storm, biting at her heels like a dog.

Tediousness creeps over her long arms like a shadow,
Or just a forbidden memory, longingly forgotten,
She starts to tremble in the chilling wind,
The cold starts to crunch,
Mist seeps from the mountaintops like a stream,
The smog floods into her eyes,
Blinding her from greed and darkness,
Shadow falls,
She feels lethargic,
Suddenly to fall into a dream,
Deeper and darker than a forest itself.

She wakes to see the realistic mirage of the sun,
She is affectionately welcomed by the wildlife,
No chill in the air to freeze her,
No darkness to riddle her,
No shadow to trick her,
Just a perpetual, endless paradise.

Matthew Gosling (10)
Mowden Junior School

The Footy King

Today at football I have to train
Tomorrow we have an important game
Against our rivals it will be war
I practise shooting, I hope I score!
The match begins, I look at goal
I pray for victory with all my soul
The crowd supports with applause and din
They shout and scream, a goal we win.

William Whittaker (9)
Mowden Junior School

Painting

With a flick
And a twirl,
A stroke
And a line

My picture
Is here,
Forever
To stay.

If you
Do dare
To scratch
Or tear,

You will
Be in
Deep trouble,
So don't!

But if
You dare
To tear
Or rip,

Then I
Will be
Forced to
Do the same to you!

So don't you
Touch
Or tear
My painting!

Marran Turner (9)
Mowden Junior School

Inside The Witch's Cauldron

Set the cauldron to boil and bake,
Stir up the liquid, stir up the meat,
Burning, battered spider's leg,
Bubbling pot, beetle's head,
Eye of frog and tail of dog,
Beak of chicken, dragon's breath,
Set the cauldron to boil and bake,
Stir up the liquid, stir up the meat.

Foot of bat and witch's hat,
Wart of frog and toe of dog,
A fresh lizard's eye and heart of a magpie,
Bubbling cauldron with beetle's head,
Set the cauldron to boil and bake,
Stir up the liquid, stir up the meat,
With smell of adults' feet,
Now the cauldron is complete.

Harriet Walker (10)
Mowden Junior School

Early Morning . . .

Early morning,
Dolphins jump,
Piranha swim,
I go down the water
See the sharks sleep
And the fish eat

I jump in
Dive down
To the bottom I go
Pulling and pulling
I reach the bottom
Fish are swimming
Sharks are eating.

Christopher Dove (11)
Mowden Junior School

Bishop Hatto And The Rats

Bishop Hatto full of fear,
Went to the River Rhine which was very near,
He climbed up into his crumbling tower,
Before the rats came full of evil power!

When the cats saw the rat coming near,
They fled from the tower full of fear,
The servants heard Bishop Hatto scream,
For the rats had made it through the stream.

When the servants opened the door,
They found Bishop Hatto lying on the floor,
His bones were spread all around
And his teeth were lying on the ground.

As the servants flew from the rats,
They heard the screech of the fearful cats,
Most of the rats had left blood and bones on the floor,
As a safe servant actually saw.

Stephanie Coates (10)
Mowden Junior School

School

Reading is my favourite thing,
But I also like to sing,
Write and write and write some more,
I didn't drop ink on the floor.

I didn't know the sun was a star,
I'm not the one who can run very far,
I never wear a bright pink top,
I didn't put her in a strop!

I always want to go to school,
Even if I break the rules,
I never get into a fight,
I only like to read and write.

Lily Thompson (9)
Mowden Junior School

In The Ring

Here comes Winter entering the ring,
Followed by Spring, who will win?
Winter the heavyweight jeering with the crowd,
Spring, the underdog's fans cheering loud,
Here is the bell, *ding, ding, ding*,
Winter Vs Spring, who will win?

Here's Winter with a left hook and with a jab,
But Spring's holding on,
He tries a left and a right hook,
But Winter is strong.

Spring's looking lively, let's see what he can do,
Here comes a left hook and there's a jab,
Winter is reeling, now's his chance,
One hook and he's won, that's all to do.

Oh no! There's a problem, will he strike the blow?
Five seconds to go, only he knows.
He's summoning the strength, here it comes,
There's a thud and a crash,

Spring has won!

Jonathan Wilkes (11)
Mowden Junior School

The Sea

The sea makes waves that go up and down
That look like a whale squirting water
The sea is blue just like a dolphin swimming in a pool
The sea is cool just like ice cream melting
The sea is really fun at the seaside
The sea is really blue and very salty
The sea is very big and you can sail on it
The sea is stormy and grey with crashing waves.

Jade Edwardson (8)
Mowden Junior School

Young Writers - Once Upon A Rhyme Co Durham

Dear Sir

Once I did something real bad
It made the teacher both angry and sad
I bought a packet of extra itch
A horribly horrible event I picked
In which the teacher went for PE
Just when we were having our school tea
And then I put it in her pants
I thought the effect would be like ants
And although the timing went horribly wrong
The powdered stuff was unequally strong
And so the teacher went through a year
With enormous lumps sticking out of her rear
But she didn't spend a day off school
So we had to do French, in which I need to be fluent
So I wrote a letter from Dad to Head saying
Dear Sir
Can I stay off instead?
Cos I'm feelin' sick,
Plez don't think my sonz
Playin' truant!

Niamh Caverhill (8)
Mowden Junior School

The Tide In The River

The tide in the river,
The tide in the river,
The tide in the river runs deep,
I saw a shiver,
Pass over the river,
As the tide turned in its sleep.
The river's deep,
The river's deep,
As it passes in its sleep.

Nathan Braithwaite (10)
Mowden Junior School

Winter

You get your coat from the closet door
And then you swap your shirt
For a jumper I mean,
You go outside and there is no dirt,
Just snow!

Then your friends come out to play
And you then go to the park,
You play until your mum shouts out,
'Come back dear, it's getting dark.'
You're upset!

You've had so much fun,
Playing a snowball fight,
Making snowmen,
While it was light,
But now, it's dark!

The snow was like paper,
The snowflakes were like God's pencil sharpenings,
The ice was like clear plastic trays,
The frost was like billions of rubber shavings,
I was so excited when I saw it!

Frances Hodgson (9)
Mowden Junior School

Winter Is . . .

Winter is a time to get wrapped up
Get food made by a cook
It's when snow falls to the ground
It makes a calm and soothing sound

With campers outside toasting marshmallows
People listening and watching the snow
The trees start to sway in the breeze
And people start to get a cold and sneeze.

Jade McGarrell (9)
Mowden Junior School

The Sad Face

The sad face is running across the border,
Wetting everything as she goes,
Her tears smashing against the rocks,
The rocks are upset, they begin to cry,
The water begins to trickle onto her,
She starts to cry even more,
Making the leaves brush along her face as she goes,
Pebbles being washing down scaring her face.

Her face scared forever,
She's even more upset, she starts to cry even more,
Her tears hurting the rocks,
Pushing the rocks under the sadness of her tears,
She starts to flood,
Crashing into the trees making them upset,
The trees drop their tears.

She starts to realise what she has done,
She apologises to the trees and starts to slow down her tears,
Apologising to the rocks,
She gently stops her tears,
Just trickling down her face gently.

Now when she gets upset,
She knows just to think of the ones she's hurting
And gently slows down into the flow again.

Hannah Smith (11)
Mowden Junior School

School

Walking down the school paths
Having lots of laughs
On the way to maths

When we do history, it's such a mystery
When we do ICT, oh dear me!

Taylor Weeks (9)
Mowden Junior School

The Tiger

I saw one, one day,
When I was on holiday
Running through the jungle,
Making a loud rumble.

It was climbing up a tree
And it suddenly pounced on me,
I ran for my life,
Praying to Christ.

I ran through the bushes
And took out my knife,
But there was no one there,
But I didn't really care.

All of a sudden I fell on the floor,
Looking up at the big thing,
It had razor-sharp pointed teeth
And I knew I was going to be beef.

I crawled into the bushes
And ran to the camp,
I locked the door
And fell down panting on the floor.

Andrew Barnes (10)
Mowden Junior School

Miss Trunchbull

Miss Trunchbull was a big, fat bull,
She never, ever got full,
She ranted and raged,
So she had to be caged,
Which she thought was so very dull.

Lauren Turner (9)
Mowden Junior School

Winter To Spring

Winter is melting and spring is blooming,
Snow fading and flowers growing,
Ice and rain disappear,
Leaves and buds on trees appear,
Winter is dying and spring is alive.

Animals come out of hibernation,
Spreading out across the nation,
The sun returns from holiday,
Maybe he'll shine every day,
Winter is going and spring is coming.

Newborn animals all around,
Snowdrops jumping from the ground,
Squirrels feasting on their winter stock,
The farmer now has a larger flock,
Winter is hibernating and spring is leaping.

James Dobson (10)
Mowden Junior School

The Train's Journey

The train pulls out of the station
Five hours behind time, better go quick
Passengers moan and groan
Some faraway clock ticks

Children walk around bored
Anxious adults look out of the carriage
Hoping to catch up on their journey
We are approaching the next station

After three days of travel
Bored humans sigh sighs of relief
They have arrived at the station
On time, all people are happy

Hip hip hooray for the train!

Declan Gegg (10)
Mowden Junior School

The Haunted Mansion

On the corner of our street,
Stands a house where my friends and I meet.
It hasn't been lived in for ages,
On the hall table an old Yellow Pages.

An old piano in the light of the moon,
My friends play though it's out of tune,
We went through the wooden door,
We couldn't see anymore.

Ghosts slipping through the floor,
Frankenstein pushing through a door,
Zombies coming from the garden,
Strange little voices saying pardon.

My friends and I go in every day,
We really can't stay away,
Just as we're about to leave,
You would never really believe.

I felt a little twitch
And I turned into a witch,
Argh!

Rebecca Wilson (9)
Mowden Junior School

Farm

Here comes the horse, clickety-clack along the track,
A competition to win, as the crowd comes in.

Here comes the cow, moo, moo, moo,
As she eats some grass as she walks past.

Here comes the chicken and the duck, quack, quack, quack,
Cluck, cluck, cluck.

Here comes the farmer, along the brook,
He's proud of his animals, the horse, the cow, the chicken and duck.

Alice Morley (8)
Mowden Junior School

The Summer Is Here

Summer day, rabbits out,
Hopping through woods,
Oh what a great day!
Looking for their prey.

Children are playing outside,
Playing football it looks like.
Oh what a great day!
Ball rolls down the hill.

The sun is out,
Shining down on the gardens.
Oh what a great day!
The sun is spreading its arms wide.

People on the beach,
Having a great time.
Oh what a great day!
Waves crashing against the rocks.

People out for picnics,
Eating lots of yummy food.
Oh what a great day!
Eating yummy cake it looks like.

The sun goes down,
The day is over,
Oh what a great day it had been,
Everyone had gone in talking about what a great day it had been!

Hannah Ferguson (10)
Mowden Junior School

My Brother

My brother is a nuisance
Every day and night
He really is a handful
And he's quite a horrible sight

My brother eats spiders
From the dirty drain
He loves to play out in the mud
Especially in the rain

He joined my school last September
And never leaves me alone
He joined Miss Shaw's class in Year 3
And spends lots of break times playing round a tree

He's quite annoying but still my brother
And I do not wish for another.

Kieran Lynch (9)
Mowden Junior School

Poems

Poems sooth
Poems smooth

Poems are jumpy
Poems are bumpy

Poems are like twilight
Poems are bright

Poems turn
Poems sometimes churn

Poems gurgle
Poems burble

Poems sometimes even explode
Bang!

Emily Ingleson (10)
Mowden Junior School

My Sister

My sister is horrible to me
And if you see her, you will soon see
That I am telling the truth
About her pushing me

My sister always gets grounded
And blames it on me
So we both get sent to bed
Without any tea

My sister has horrible feet
They smell like rotten cheese
And when she puts them in front of my face
They're so horrible they make me sneeze

My sister shouts all the time
She gets told off
And then calms down
Then she walks off and goes into town.

Kerry Holliday (10)
Mowden Junior School

The Sound Of The Abbey

In a deep faraway ancient abbey,
There is a big vast space,
It is very icy and cold,
Lost in time day by day,
The smell of fresh air covers every space,
Sheep bleating all around us,
Loud footsteps everywhere,
Rustling leaves and swaying trees,
Water flowing, nature all around us,
Everything stopped,
The choir monks are here,
Only silence can be heard.

Caitlin Stalker (9)
Mowden Junior School

Our Teacher Is A Ghost

Our teacher is a ghost,
She glides around the room,
She's weird, spooky, scary
And is the colour of doom.

The teacher floats around,
Looking at our books,
If we do it wrong,
She leaves us with the spooks.

When she goes through the wall,
We all think she is gone,
But when we hear a scream,
We know we're very wrong.

When the school bell starts to ring
And it is time to go home,
The teacher flies away,
To her weird, spooky dome.

Samantha Corner (10)
Mowden Junior School

Mind

In my mind I can hide
Anything I want
It covers up my deepest secrets
Secrets I would never share with anyone
Else but me

I keep in my mind
A series of notes
To prompt myself with what I do

In my mind
I can keep
My opinion of things I like
Things I don't.

Grace Edwards (10)
Mowden Junior School

Football Dreaming

All day I have a picture,
In my mind,
It is so exciting,
I'm not even listening to the teacher,
All day I twist and turn,
I do no work,
I start to dream,
About the team,
Bend it like Beckham?
No! No! No!
I shoot it like Shearer,
I dribble like Dyer,
I run like Robert,
I work hard like Woodgate,
I jump high like Jenas
And I speed like Speed,
I'm man of the match!
'Jack Whittaker! Get on with your work or . . .'
'Sorry Mr White.'
So I start to write.

Jack Whittaker (10)
Mowden Junior School

The Playground Rap

In the playground you can play a card game,
All be friends
Or call each other names.
You could get some extra studying done
Or have a game of tig
For endless fun.
But when the bell rings,
One thing's for sure,
You won't be out again for an hour or more.

Keziah Morley (10)
Mowden Junior School

What Is Yellow?

Yellow is the sun shining bright
Bringing lots of light.
Yellow is a thousand grains of sand.
The shiny cymbals of a band.
Yellow is a buttercup,
The happy feeling of a newborn pup.
Yellow is the stripe of bees
And my teddy which I always want to squeeze.
Yellow is lumpy custard
And spicy mustard.
Yellow like butter -
You take one lick and you're a nutter!
Yellow is the middle of a daisy
Which blows around in the wind like crazy.
Yellow is lovely blonde hair
Streaming out when you ride at the fair.
Yellow is a golden eagle
(Hunting these is illegal).
Yellow faces aren't feeling happy
When they have to change a baby's nappy!
Yellow is a happy colour - no doubt about it
But can you imagine living without it?

Louise Bracken (8)
Mowden Junior School

The Fat Panther

The fat panther is very, very fat,
The fat panther is very, very slow,
The fat panther is very, very . . .
Oh no! Got to go . . . !

Hannah Dennis (8)
Mowden Junior School

A to Z

A is for Anne who is cool
B is for Ben who likes to rule
C is for Charlie who loves animals
D is for David who's into fossils
E is for Emma who is always being silly
F is for Frances, her baby sister is Milly
G is for Gary who picks his nose
H is for Hannah who touches her toes
 I is for Ian who loves to read a book
J is for Jodie who is learning to cook
K is for Kathryn who is very good at sport
L is for Luke who is never caught
M is for Matty who loves ice cream
N is for Nick who is in a daydream
O is for Owen who is great at football
P is for Pat who shops at the mall
Q is for Queeney who is having a doze
R is for Rachel who is proud of her nose
S is for Sandy who all people like
T is for Ted who's best friend is Mike
U is for Una who chases the boys
V is for Vicky who makes a lot of noise
W is for Will who always has fun
X is for Xania who wears her hair in a bun
Y is for Yelle, he likes to yell
Z is for Zorhah who has got a silver bell.

Charlotte Foster (9)
Mowden Junior School

The Night Fright Ghost

You know when you're lying in your bed
And you get the feeling someone is there
But don't you worry, it's just the night fright *ghost*

He comes and bites you round your neck
And he may have a go at your head
But don't you worry, it's just the night fright *ghost*

He might rip all your hair out
And gobble your arm right off
But don't you worry, it's just the night fright *ghost*

He'll probably take you down to his basement
For his lunch
But don't you worry, it's only the night fright *ghost*

He'll come and nibble off your fingers
And that's not bad because you don't have to work
But don't you worry, it's just the night fright *ghost*

Just scream and shout, he'll go away
So you don't have to worry
But if he's there, don't worry, it's just the night fright *ghost*

So while you're waiting in your bed for morning to arrive
Don't worry if you hear a bump
It's just the night fright ghost.

Lucy O'Neill (9)
Mowden Junior School

Wolf

Twinkling, sparkling, shining eyes,
Within them lies
The fire of one's desire.

Bloodstained, jagged, razor-sharp fangs,
Its owner hunts in quite large gangs,
Chomping, chewing, biting and tearing.

Curved, retractable, lethal claws,
They add to the fear of his gaping jaws,
Run, chase, slash and smash.

White, silvery, glittering fur,
Acts as a kind of enchanting lure,
Leading prey to their death, away.

Wolf, fearsome and lethal might,
Stalking in the darkest night,
Filling everything with shaking fright.

Andrew Page (10)
Mowden Junior School

Snow Is . . .

Snow is a
White fluffy polar bear lying across the land
Snow is a
White cloth floating down to Earth
Snow is
Clouds softly falling from the sky
Snow is
Sugar sprinkled on the rooftops
Snow is
Confetti thrown into the sky
Snow is
Milk poured onto the land
Snow is
Feathers falling to the ground.

Kathryn Binks (9)
Mowden Junior School

The Unicorn

(In loving memory of Grandad)

I was lonely and sad,
everyone thought I was mad.
I was short on smiles and laughs,
even my teacher said I was not good at maths.

Then the unicorn came to me out of the blue,
I actually got to see one it's true.
There he stood pure white in the bright moonlight,
his hooves jet-black, his eyes as gold as honey,
my day had suddenly turned sunny.

His mane flowed like simmering milk,
his tail glittered like silver silk.
The famous horn sparkled with dancing fire,
I became as stiff as hard wire as he spoke to me poetically,
'You're surrounded by friends, have faith,
your work will soon be on the mend.'

Then just as quickly as he first came to me,
he vanished, I was speechless and mystified.

There are special creatures born every new dawn,
but there's nothing as magical as a unicorn.

Becky Mutton (9)
Mowden Junior School

Arrested

I did something naughty
I didn't realise the police were watching me
They've caught me
Oh no I have to leg it
I leg it down the path
Don't know where to go
I go in a direction
I don't really know
So I just carry on running
I am lost, I hide somewhere
Where they cannot find me
The police go in a completely different direction
They have lost me, phew . . .
I am exhausted
I then climb out and I look around
I cannot see them anywhere
They find me
They scare me!
Oh no, I have to let it again
But oh no . . .
Both directions are blocked, now I 'm caught
I know what will happen
I'll get taken to court
Guess what? Now I am in *big trouble!*

Rebecca Bynoe (9)
Mowden Junior School

I Wish I Could Be, But I am Glad That I'm Me

I wish I was a bird to fly over the world.
I wish I was a dolphin to leap over the ocean.
I wish I was a crab to crawl in the sea.
I wish I was a monkey to swing from tree to tree.
I wish I was a sheep so I could keep warm in winter.
I wish I was a butterfly, so colourful and free.
I wish I was a snake to slide all over the place.
I wish I was a rabbit so I could eat all the carrots.
I wish I was a frog to leap over the pond.
I wish I was a cat so I could sit near the fire all day.
I wish I was a crocodile so I could go *snap, snap, snap!*
I wish I was a hippy so I could play in muddy water.
I wish I was a spider so I could make sparkling webs.
I wish I was a starfish to float on the sea.
I wish I was a chameleon so I could change colour.
I wish I was a fish so I could swim under the sea.
I wish I was a humming bird so I could hum all day.
I wish I was a grizzly bear so I could hibernate all winter.
I wish I was a deer, so friendly and kind.
I wish I was a kangaroo so I could jump around all day.
I wish I was a pig so I could slush in the mud all day.
I wish I was a hen so I could peck at corn all day.
I wish I was a turtle so I could go at my own pace.
I wish I was a hare so I could win the race.
I wish I was a cheetah so I could be the fastest in the world.
I wish I was an elephant so I could soak you with my trunk.
I wish I was a dove and be with the one I love.
I wish I was a duck so I could go *quack, quack, quack!*
I wish I was a gorilla, so strong and big.
I wish I was a giraffe to reach the top of the tree,
But I am so glad that I am me!

Yasmin Peckitt-Singh (8)
Mowden Junior School

Kielder Forest

She rocks gently in the wind,
Back and forth,
Back and forth,
Creeping slowly outwards every second,
Whistling in the breeze.

Mesmerising those who dare enter,
Casting them under her enchantment,
Sending them into a dream world,
Gloominess outstretches over her,
Like butter spreading on toast,
Light disappears from her essence,
All is dark and enthralling,
The eerie silence filling her.

At the crack of dawn,
The light shall come flooding the forest,
She will be still with a pleasant awe,
Then once again people come walking on her beauty,
Her loveliness spreading further every day,
She sways once again,
But now she is tempered,
Small children climb her trunk,
Destroying her unsuspectingly,
Without a notice.

Jenny Stalker (11)
Mowden Junior School

Seasons

Wintertime, the trees are bare,
Plants asleep everywhere,
Fir trees green, berries red,
Squirrels asleep, gone to bed.

Spring, earth warms up, bulbs appear,
Blackbirds sing, can you hear?
Daffodils, snowdrops, crocuses too,
Yellow, white, pink and blue.

Summertime, afternoon teas,
Apple trees, bumblebees,
Pretty gardens, perfume perfection,
Bubbling streams catch your reflection.

Autumn, when trees turn gold,
Days turn shorter, getting cold,
Plants are sleepy, squirrels eat nuts,
Heating comes on, heats all of us.

Shaun Gault (11)
Mowden Junior School

The Wind

I can lash out like a whip when mad
And yet whistle like an old sailor.

I can creep through an open window
And howl like an injured dog.

I can rummage through a garden like a burglar
And hurt people by pushing them over.

I can glide like a swallow
And shove baby birds when flying.

I can spray a field with the scent of lavender
And injure a child.

Christopher Wiseman (10)
Ouston Junior School

Up In The Loft . . . Down In The Basement . . .

Up in the loft there's . . .

A Christmas tree,
Old Hallowe'en clothes,
Babies toys,
Old photos of my mother's pose,
Old toys that were my father's
And an . . .
Old garden hose.

Down in the basement there's . . .

Old bricks,
A rusty bike,
Slates from the roof,
A small bike,
Wood from the banister
And . . .
Two smelly old boots that my father wore to hike!

Rachel Laidler (10)
Ouston Junior School

The Cat

While the night wind blows,
He waits, perched on a wall,
Waits for the bird to fly past
And land on the road,
Sharp claws grip the wall,
Green eyes stare at the prey,
Brown fur spikes up,
As if he has got an electric shock.

As fast as a cheetah,
He dances and pounces on his prey,
Chews it to its skeleton,
As he goes to rest
For the night.

Kay Pearson (11)
Ouston Junior School

Peace

Peace is the colour of white
Peace smells like the countryside
Peace tastes like fruit
Peace sounds like a swan
Calmly floating down a stream
Peace feels like relaxation
Peace lives in the countryside.

Kyle Wilson (9)
Ouston Junior School

War

War is mouldy green.
War smells like pain and death.
War tastes like fresh blood dripping from the body.
War sounds like gunfire, crying and bombing.
War feels like you're next door to death.
War lives in a soggy trench.

Daniel Empson (10)
Ouston Junior School

Peace

Peace is colourful
It smells like happiness
Peace tastes like chocolate
It sounds like singing birds
It feels like a flower ready to shoot up
Peace lives in a rainbow.

Amy Marsden (9)
Ouston Junior School

Hope

Hope is yellow
It smells like fresh flowers
Hope tastes like vanilla ice cream
It sounds like a gentle voice
Hope feels like you're happy
Hope lives inside our hearts.

Bethany Findlay (10)
Ouston Junior School

Winter

W intertime is here
I cy roads, you better go slow
N ew Year's Eve is coming soon
T rees are bare and animals sleep
E lves help Santa get the presents
R udolph's nose shines Santa's way.

Lauren Andrews (9)
Ouston Junior School

Wealth

Wealth is yellow like gold shining in the sun
It smells like sweet metal money
Wealth tastes like an all-you-can-eat buffet
It sounds like money clashing together
Wealth feels like cold hard cash
It lives in a rich person's house.

Andrew Mollett (10)
Ouston Junior School

The Wind

When the wind is raging through the tangled forest,
It is a charging bull flattening everything in its path.
When the wind is gently swaying through the grass,
It is a quiet ladybird hovering from flower to flower.
When the wind is roaring through buildings,
It is a fierce lion catching its prey.
When the wind is silently whispering,
It is a pixie casting spells.
When the wind is screeching above the hilltops,
It is a cackling witch bringing evil.

Katrina Small (11)
Ouston Junior School

Cruelty

Cruelty is as black as the night sky.
It smells like acid burning through people.
It tastes of blood pouring out of a sheep killed by man.
Cruelty sounds like woodlands getting chopped down
And animals losing their homes.
It feels like a torture so horrible, no man could survive,
It lives in the heart of man.

Lilyanna Turner (9)
Ouston Junior School

War

War is red,
It smells like fear,
War tastes like scalding iron,
It sounds like crying soldiers,
It feels slimy and greasy,
War lives in your mind.

Adam Kirkup (10)
Ouston Junior School

Pain

Pain is light grey like heavy clouds in the sky,
Pain smells like sewers, it's as strong as thunder,
Pain tastes like slime which is as green as the grass,
Pain sounds like a man and a gun meeting at the heart,
Pain feels like a splinter going deep within your body,
Pain lives at the very top of Mount Everest
Slowly coming down to get . . .
Who knows!

Brogan Stephenson (10)
Ouston Junior School

Peace

Peace is just like the sky
It smells like fresh flowers in the springtime
It tastes like a sugary rose petal drink
It sounds like a piano playing a lullaby gently
It feels calm like a swan gliding across the calm gentle sea
Peace lives in the heart of Heaven.

Mikki Clark (9)
Ouston Junior School

Autumn

Leaves zoom through the sky like a jet
People out for berry week
Animals go to sleep in trees
Spider webs sparkle like silver
The moon so bright it lights the night
Comes too soon.

Adam Rowe (8)
Ouston Junior School

The Wind

I can go calmly through the flowers without waking them.
I can attack ships till they sink.
I can dodge past buildings quick as a flash
And glide sneakily through keyholes.
I can be rough and ferocious
And blow your house down.
I can charge at the cliff like an angry bull.
I can smash windows with all my power.
I can be a dragon angry and furious.
I can roar and howl but I can take leaves off trees like feathers.

Harpreet Singh Jhally (10)
Ouston Junior School

Calm

Calm is gentle like the sea
It's like a raindrop rolling down your body
Calm is music playing gently across the drifting sea
It tastes like honey.

Shonagh Glass (10)
Ouston Junior School

Hate

Hate is black
It smells like smoke
It tastes like a burnt crumpet
It sounds like a lion roaring
It feels like a slimy snake
It lives in a pitch-black cave.

Ryan Edgar (10)
Ouston Junior School

Spooky

As I opened the door,
This is what I saw . . .
Chains rattling,
Blood dripping,
Spiders crawling,
Bats sleeping,
Windows smashed,
Doors creaking,
Zombies moaning,
Mice squeaking,
Black cats screeching,
People screaming,
Shadows groaning,
I ran away!
Did you?

Liam Twomey (8)
Ouston Junior School

Scary Poem

Up the creaking stairs
There sat some cats on rocking chairs
Witches fly away at night
When you meet them, you'll get a fright
Howls and growls fading away
An old werewolf turning grey
Squeaking and squealing red-eyed rats
Who live in old witches' hats
Ghosts drifting around the room
Echoing voices saying *'Doom!'*

Abbie Carr (9)
Ouston Junior School

On The Beach

I'm on the beach,
Sitting down,
Listening, looking all around,
The beaming sun in my eyes
And seaweed on my feet.

I'm on the beach,
Sitting down,
Listening, looking all around,
Laughing, giggling is what I hear
And the sea crashing against the rocks.

I'm on the beach,
Sitting down,
Listening, looking all around,
Girls and boys picking up shells,
Seagulls cry as they soar through the sky.

Gemma Heron (9)
Ouston Junior School

Scary Poem

I'm in my bed,
Clock strikes 12, I opened my curtains,
This is what I saw . . .
Tarantulas crawling,
Vampires approaching,
Giant spiders,
Ghosts haunting,
This is what I heard . . .
Howling at the full moon,
Hooting in my ear,
Rattling of chains,
I awoke struggling for breath,
Hallelujah, it was only a dream.

Kate Driver (9)
Ouston Junior School

Spooky

In the night this is what I hear . . .
Dogs barking
Cats purring
Doors slamming
Gates rattling
Am I dreaming? No!

In the night this is what I see . . .
Smoke out of the chimney pots
Birds flying
Black cats
Gates and werewolves
Is this a dream? No!

In the night this is what I feel . . .
A cold breeze
A dagger in my arm
A brick on my leg
A spider up my back
Is this a dream? Yes!

Ben Holden (9)
Ouston Junior School

Winter

Children love snowy days
Children slipping on the path
Sledging down the hilltops

Adults hate kids slipping all over the place
Throwing snowballs at their windows

Snow trickling down on our heads.

Daniel Hawthorne (8)
Ouston Junior School

Spooky In My Bedroom

It's pitch-black,
I'm in my bedroom,
The curtains start flapping,
I hear screaming,
A horrible cackle,
That's it, I hide under my quilt,
I try to make myself stop imagining things,
Shadows start to howl,
Having parties on my wall,
I hold my cuddly tight,
The door slams,
I get so frightened, I go to sleep,
I wake up the next morning,
All I have now are the nightmares
And feathers that grow on my face.

Sophie Taylor (9)
Ouston Junior School

While I Was Asleep

I was in my bedroom fast asleep,
When the clock struck 12,
I woke all of a sudden,
With a crack of a tile,
I was scared.

With a hoot of an owl,
I was shaking and my teeth clashing together,
With doors creaking and smashing,
I heard thunder in the sky,
With a flash of lightning the sky lit up,
I was scared . . .

Don't walk . . . run!

Amy Kingston (8)
Ouston Junior School

Summer Under The Sea

Under the sea,
Where fish can come up and talk to me,
The sun shines all day,
Breeze blows all cares away,
This is summer under the sea!

Under the sea,
It's a holiday where there's no sign of mozzies,
Just swarms of krill,
You'll enjoy it, you will,
Your holiday under the sea!

Under the sea,
You could have free fish for tea!
Just swimming along,
There is nothing wrong,
With a holiday under the sea,
Hey!

Charlotte Hogg (9)
Ouston Junior School

Winnie The Pooh's Problem

The bear called Winnie the Pooh
Said one day,
'Oh, what can I do?
There's no honey here,
Well, oh dear,
Sorry, no honey for you.'

The same bear, Winnie the Pooh,
Said the next day,
'I've got news for you!
The honey has gone,
Now I know what's wrong -
I ate it all one afternoon.'

Katie Hampson (10)
Ouston Junior School

The Owl

Fields of a forest
Are swaying in the cold night breeze,
The claws begin to move,
It has awoken.

Big beady eyes scan the earth,
Looking for bait,
For it is hungry,
From sleeping all day.

Long strong wings,
Leap into the air,
Motion is spotted,
Down he goes to eat his feast.

Eyes like an eagle,
Helps in the night,
Quicker than a jet,
He swoops and wins.

The feast is over,
So now he can sleep,
Until the next night,
He shall rest.

Lois Bridgewood (11)
Ouston Junior School

Fear

Fear is as white as a cloud
Fear is the smell of aftershave
It tastes of soft bread with butter on
It sounds like the wind swirling about
It feels like an assassin is coming to kill you
It lives in the heart of a rock.

Alexander Rowe (10)
Ouston Junior School

Happiness

Happiness is yellow like the steaming sun
It smells like runny, sloppy egg yolk
It tastes like delicious Christmas pudding
It sounds like dripping lolly
Happiness feels like the love of wonder
Happiness lives inside us!

Samantha Bright (9)
Ouston Junior School

War

War is blood-red spurting from wounds
It smells like black smoky gunpowder
It tastes of death and revenge
It sounds of bombs exploding and cries of pain
It feels like the earth will no longer be there!
It lives in the heart of jealousy and hate.

Nathan Cooper (10)
Ouston Junior School

Happiness

Happiness is as white as a cloud
It smells of people doing joyful things
It tastes like delicious eggs and bacon
It sounds like birds singing beautifully
It feels like the sun shining on you
Happiness lives in the air.

Dean Smith (9)
Ouston Junior School

Death

Death is the colour of a bloodstream
Death smells like rotting flesh
Death tastes like poison from a cobra
Death sounds like screaming in the dusty air
Death feels like blood trickling down your back
Death lives inside a very sharp dagger.

Sarah Currie (9)
Ouston Junior School

Anger!

Anger is the colour of blood
Anger smells like a burning house
Anger tastes like someone has just put a ball of fire in your mouth
Anger sounds like an erupting volcano
Anger feels like you have just been stabbed several times
Anger lives in a roaring fire.

Christopher Hunter (9)
Ouston Junior School

Pain

Pain is a dark blunt red.
Pain smells like a rotten apple.
It tastes like crunchy sand dried up.
Pain sounds like wolves howling in the night.
It feels like rough sandpaper.
It can live inside you.

Andrew Spurr (9)
Ouston Junior School

Fear

Fear is grass-green
It smells like old coal burning from a fire
Fear tastes like warm water running down your throat
It sounds like a thunderstorm bouncing off the ground
Fear feels like water absorbing into your body
Fear lives in the heart of your soul.

Rachel Cockburn (10)
Ouston Junior School

War

War is army-green
It smells like muddy grass
War tastes like burnt metal plates
It sounds like a volcano erupting
It feels bumpy, sharp and hot
War lives in the heart of a battlefield.

Katie McGuire (9)
Ouston Junior School

Peace

Peace is white
It smells like calm air
Peace tastes like white snow
It sounds like nothing, it's so quiet
Peace feels like the beautiful morning sky
It lives at home.

Bethany Cockburn (9)
Ouston Junior School

Peace

Peace is as white as a dove
It smells like honey in a jar
Peace tastes like jam on a piece of toast
Peace sounds like silent violins
It feels like gentle air
Peace lives in a heart of a dove.

Jessica Morrow (10)
Ouston Junior School

Fear

Fear is black
Fear smells like gunpowder exploding
Fear tastes like blood dripping
It sounds like trees snapping
It feels like being shot
It lives in the heart of Hell.

Bradley Gray (10)
Ouston Junior School

War

War is dull green
It smells like a bomb explosion
War tastes like a rotten tomato
It sounds like fireworks exploding
War feels like stabbing daggers
It lives in the heart of fighting lions.

Sophie Patterson (9)
Ouston Junior School

Mystical Flight

It was resting in the darkness
Awoke from the frosty air
A little girl in her bedroom
Sleeping in her mind
As it began its mystical flight

It watched the glowing moonlight
And followed the guiding path
It saw the sealed window
Showing the small figure
As it continued its mystical flight

The sleeping child still dreaming
The magical fantasy
The magic swirls around the air
As the little girl still dreaming
The mystical magic travelled
To end its mystical flight!

Samantha Brown (11)
Ouston Junior School

Autumn Leaves

I run over the rough grass
The leaves crunch under my feet
The wind blows the leaves off the trees
And leaves the trees bare
The leaves dance in the breeze
Happy to be free
That's what I see

I open my window as leaves get blown in
Tired and restless
After their night through.

Olivia Douglass (8)
Ouston Junior School

We've Won The Cup

We've won the World Cup
Hooray for England
It was deafening
In the sold-out crowd
Everyone on their feet
Cheering for England
'Sweet chariot'

We've won the World Cup
Hooray for England
Jonny Wilko kicking
Jason Robinson scoring
And everybody going wild
As Martin Johnson holding
The golden cup

We've won the World Cup
Hooray for England
They powered through the stages
Beating Samoa, France and Georgia
And now we've beat Australia
What a celebration
We've won the cup!

Adam Hunt (10)
Ouston Junior School

Frustration

Frustration is red
It smells like burning fire
Frustration tastes sour
It sounds like fireworks
It feels clingy and sticky
Frustration lives inside me!

Emma Luker (9)
Ouston Junior School

9/11

It was a beautifully warm and sunny day
In New York City
And then *bang!*
Screams of terror
Cries of pain
The yells of people jumping out of windows
People running, panicking, hiding
Smoke covering streets and everywhere fire!
And then *bang!*
The second plane hits
Burning buildings
Smoke everywhere
People crying, cowering
And then *bang!*
The first tower implodes
More terror, screams
Aeroplane passengers dying
And then *bang!*
The second tower implodes
And all around
Death!
Everywhere was unearthly silent
And everywhere *death!*

Helen Briggs (10)
Ouston Junior School

Hope!

Hope is whiter than the whitest white,
It smells like a giant flower,
It tastes like a heaping bowl of sugar,
It sounds fluttery, gentle and quiet,
It feels hard but softer than wool,
Hope lives in the most unknown place.

Stephen Mollett (10)
Ouston Junior School

Death!

Death is as black as night,
It smells of rotting flesh and dead bodies,
Death tastes of burning wood and hot ashes,
It sounds like someone scraping their nails across a blackboard,
Death feels like broken glass and sharp rocks,
Death lives in the heart of a big dark wood.

Rachael Yeadon (10)
Ouston Junior School

Hate

Hate is the colour of darkest ash,
It smells like poisonous gases streaming into a dark room,
Hate has the taste of the most bitter lemon,
It sounds like howling wind whistling through the trees,
It feels like hot splintered iron,
Hate lives in our darkest fears.

Jack Thirlwell (10)
Ouston Junior School

Kindness

Kindness is gold - it's priceless,
Kindness smells like the sweetest roses ever discovered,
Kindness tastes like freshly picked strawberries from the finest bush,
It feels like a soft gentle breeze blowing against your face,
Kindness lives in Heaven.

Simon Tyrrell (10)
Ouston Junior School

War!

War is a black cloud
War smells like a dusty town that's had a hurricane come past
War tastes like blood splatting all over the ground
War sounds like people dying and bombs landing on buildings
War feels like fire and rock flying all over the place
War lives inside your mind.

Daniel Nicholson (9)
Ouston Junior School

Hope

Hope is where the sun shines down on you,
It smells like fresh air,
Hope tastes like fresh flowers from the ground,
It sounds like singing birds,
It feels like happiness all around you,
Hope lives inside your heart.

Rachael Miley (9)
Ouston Junior School

Anger

Anger is red like blood in your body,
It smells like smoke from a train,
It tastes like burnt toast in a grill,
It sounds like lightning in the sky,
It feels like sharp metal,
Anger lives in the heart of an explosion.

Phillip Pearson (9)
Ouston Junior School

War!

War is black and full of danger
It smells like smoke from the battlefield
It tastes like blood coming out of your body
It sounds like loud gunfire from tanks
It feels like fear coming down your spine
It lives in the pits of Hell.

Kris Bambynek (10)
Ouston Junior School

Anger!

Anger is red
It smells like burning gas
Anger tastes like bitter lemon
It sounds like the noise of a tank bombing
It feels like a shiver down your spine
Anger lives in you.

Alex Moody (10)
Ouston Junior School

Death!

Death is red, the colour of blood,
Death smells like rotten eggs,
Death tastes like green fungus,
Death sounds like an explosion,
Death feels like an electric shock,
Death lives in the hottest volcano.

Laura Kerry (10)
Ouston Junior School

Fear!

Fear is a moulded maroon,
It smells like something burning,
Fear tastes like red-hot pepper,
It sounds like a fork scraping along a plate,
Fear feels crunchy and sharp like autumn leaves,
It lives in the heart of a lion.

Laura McDermott (10)
Ouston Junior School

War!

War is lava red
It smells like fresh blood
It tastes like death and torn skin
It sounds like the stabbing of a sword
It feels rough and gungy
War lives at the very tip of a sword.

Samuel Johnson (10)
Ouston Junior School

Death!

Death is red dripping blood.
It smells like fire.
It tastes like fresh blood.
It sounds like people bursting out in tears.
Death lives in a volcano.

Jonathan Forster (10)
Ouston Junior School

Death!

Death is black,
Death smells like slithering smoke,
Death tastes like off-dated chicken,
Death sounds like a really strong snowstorm,
Death feels like water drowning you,
Death lives in the darkness of Hell.

Robyn Clark (9)
Ouston Junior School

War!

War is red,
It smells like rotten bodies in a desert,
It tastes like bitter milk,
It sounds like men shouting help in pain,
It feels like getting cut by a knife,
It lives in a graveyard.

Andrew Ellison (9)
Ouston Junior School

Fear!

Fear is blue
Smells like burnt pizza
It tastes bitty and burnt
Fear sounds like a scream from miles away
Fear feels like a broken toy.

Danielle Gleadhill (9)
Ouston Junior School

Someone Told Anna

Someone told Anna it was going to snow
Someone told Amy, Anna would know
Someone told Charlotte it was going to rain
Someone told James to catch a train
Someone told Chris there would be wind
Someone told Ryan his hair needed to be trimmed.

Anna Drake (9)
Ouston Junior School

War!

War is red blood from a wounded soldier.
It smells of dust after explosions.
War tastes of mud and dust.
It sounds like gunfire in an open battlefield.
It feels hard and sharp.
War lives in the heart of a battlefield.

Matthew Laybourn (10)
Ouston Junior School

Winter

W inter is so dull when the night falls
 I ce sparkles with Mr Jack Frost
N atural trees so bare as you walk
T alented people got so much ammo for snowballs
E xtraordinary trees look down at you in the dark
R eindeer comes down on your roof while Santa drops
   from your chimney.

Richard Young (9)
Ouston Junior School

On A Gloomy Night

When the night has come
And the moon is full,
In the misty shadows,
It's all pitch-black,
I'm all alone.
The wind is moving,
An angry, grey man,
In a long black cloak
Appears in the clouds,
How fast he can ride on a horse of fire,
Riding about till he's out of sight,
Then a long, deep scream
In the clouds of night.

Olivia Bradbury (8)
Ouston Junior School

Autumn

Autumn time is here,
The leaves begin to fall from trees
And the flowers start to die,
The moon begins to get spooky for Hallowe'en.

Jennifer Waite (8)
Ouston Junior School

Autumn

Autumn time is here
Leaves turn golden
Conkers fall
Autumn.

Jessica Guy (8)
Ouston Junior School

Spooky Night

I was in my bed, the clock struck 12
And I heard a funny noise
I looked out of my window and this is what I saw . . .

Snakes hissing,
Wolves howling,
Owls hooting,
Windows crashing,
Doors creaking,
Lightning flashing,
Witches cackling,
Dogs barking,
Creatures humming,
Cobwebs glistening,
Monsters groaning,
Wind chimes screeching,
Chains rattling,
Bats circling!
I was scared
Were you?

Amy Murray (9)
Ouston Junior School

The Evil Knight

The knight is evil as he rides through the towns,
The horse has thick red eyes like fire, as it transports the knight,
The helmet lies on him like cement that never moves,
His blade is as sharp as a giant spike,
It destroys anything in its path,
But if you want a fight, be warned, he's as strong as a boulder.

Philip Brown (9)
Ouston Junior School

Hope

Hope is white, the colour of a swan,
It smells of sweet perfume,
Hope tastes fresh and sweet,
It sounds like an acorn falling,
It feels like water woven into material,
Hope lives in the heart of every living person.

Emmy Brown (10)
Ouston Junior School

Health

Health is yellow
It smells all bright and sunny
It tastes like lovely jelly sweets
It sounds like a countryside
It feels all cool and sleepy
It lives in your inside.

Jessica Anderson (9)
Ouston Junior School

Love!

Love is colourful,
It smells like a nice summer's day,
It tastes like a chocolate cake,
It sounds like church bells ringing,
It feels like happiness,
Love lives in your heart.

Charlotte Slaymaker (9)
Ouston Junior School

The Journey Of The River

First I came from the blue sky,
Like a rocket,
A hundred miles an hour,
Splash!
The water went on somebody's eyelash,
Like a spray of water,
Twisting, curving like a snake.

Bigger and bigger the water started to flow,
Oh no! It's the waterfall.
Ahhhhh! Splash!
A little more distance before it reaches the sea,
I wonder when I will be evaporated by the sun.

Ram Prasana Jambulingam (10)
Raventhorpe Preparatory School

A Chilly Night

A chilly night, a snowy morn,
The frost bites on a magical dawn.
The children rush outside to play,
They have waited all year for today.
Hats, scarves and gloves are found,
The snow has formed a glistening mound.
The snow cannot last forever,
Don't blame me, blame the weather.
Now the snow has begun to run,
The slush cannot give us any fun.

Debbie Cheesbrough (11)
Raventhorpe Preparatory School

The River

Out of the mountain
I trickle
Descending more, more and more,
Shooting, darting,
Out I pour, pour and pour,
Sparkling, glittering,
I drag along mud,
Over the big boulders
I thud,
Dashing, splashing,
I spray,
Glistening,
I don't know the way,
Oh no!
A waterfall
Cascades,
Really, really tall,
Over the side I go,
Foamy,
Deep, deep, deep,
Over the big boulders,
I creep, creep, creep,
Meandering,
Wide, wide, wide,
Swelling,
Glide, glide, glide,
I'm there,
My journey's ended.

Adam Matthews (10)
Raventhorpe Preparatory School

River

Drip drop, drip drop!
I am starting as a spring,
Drip drop, drip drop,
As I fall I sing.

Splashing, spraying,
Down the stream I go,
Splashing, spraying,
Bubbling as I flow.

Dashing, splashing,
Over rocks and boulders.
Dashing, splashing,
Spraying at their shoulders.

I can see the sea,
I dash and I splash and say,
'Yippee!'
The journey's at an end now.

Victoria Richardson (10)
Raventhorpe Preparatory School

Snow

Snow is falling through the night
Covering everything in a glittery white
Falling past the windowpane
Covering the deserted lane

Children playing in the snow
Noses red, cheeks aglow
Building a snowman by the hedge
Speeding down the hill on a sledge

The snow begins to fall hard
Children rush out of the yard
People shelter from the storm
Rush inside to keep warm.

Cheryl Gartland (11)
Raventhorpe Preparatory School

Building A Snowman

I went into the garden and started on my snowman,
I started on the bottom, round and white.

I stood it in the middle next to my brother's big and bold.

Then it started to crumble down like leaves falling, I piled it up again.
Now for the head, it started as a very small ball, I rolled and rolled,
I could see it grow and grow and I placed it on the top.

Then I found a hat, scarf and a carrot for a nose,
Quickly I hurried back and saw it glistening in the white background,
I pushed his eyes on, then the hat
And strangled him with a scarf.
I searched for my snowman's arms,
Then I found them and stabbed them in his side.
There, he is finished,
I ran in to have my tea and scrambled up to bed.

I woke up bright and early,
I looked out of my window but all I saw
Was a pile of snow, carrot, hat and scarf.

Harriet Peacock (11)
Raventhorpe Preparatory School

Food

'I ate some yellow mustard
And then some yellow custard,'
Said little Polly Perkins.
'It was nice with rice,'
Said Goldilocks to
The three bears.
'Come and sit upon these chairs,'
Then little Jack Horner
Left his corner
To visit the puss in the well
And all the nursery characters
Sang ding dong dell!

Alexandra Thompson (9)
Raventhorpe Preparatory School

Building A Snowman

The white snow looks like a quilt.
Rolling, starting to make its body.
Bigger, bigger it grows.
We roll it into place.

We start on its head,
Starting with a tiny snowball.
Rolling, growing bigger.
We lift it on the body.
For the eyes we use two oranges.
For the nose a carrot
And for the mouth some stones.
There, we have finished the snowman,
We leave it for the night.

In the morning he is melting,
His head is getting smaller.
When we came back from school,
He was all gone into a puddle,
The oranges, carrots and stones are on the floor.

Victoria Whitaker (10)
Raventhorpe Preparatory School

Snow

Snow covers up the ground,
Like a blanket covering a bed,
Falling in big white snow drops,
Just like feathers from the sky.

Lying on the ground the snow so soft,
All the children playing,
Ten snowmen in the making
And the snowballs have just been made.

As the sun comes back to us,
The snow is quickly melting,
It's almost gone so we go in,
To sit next to the fire.

Hannah Hillary (11)
Raventhorpe Preparatory School

The River

I am a tiny trickle,
Running,
I am stunning.
I am a crashing and bashing, dashing, splashing,
Flying, shining river.
Danger for strangers if they come near,
Now a waterfall . . .
I shoot over rocks and splash, splash, splash!
I wash the soil away.
I twirl and shine like a pearl,
I curl and whirl gently,
I slowly reach the sea,
I am at my journey's end.

Danielle Overfield (10)
Raventhorpe Preparatory School

The Tumblers

The tumblers are mumblers
They cannot talk
They grumble and rumble
And tumble and mumble
Their names are Humble, Bumble and Crumble
When they try to speak
It's nonsense and jumble
The tumblers are mumblers
They cannot talk
They grumble and rumble
And tumble and mumble.

Oliver Whitchurch (9)
Raventhorpe Preparatory School

The Alien

His arms were orange
His legs were red
When his spaceship landed
I turned and fled
He followed me across a river and over a hill
My heart was racing and wouldn't be still
He finally caught me
And took me away
I was so frightened
I started to pray
We went in his spacecraft
Flew over a stream
But then I woke up -
It was only a dream.

James Mitchinson (10)
Raventhorpe Preparatory School

My Wish

If I had a wish,
I'd wish to fly.
I'd glide through the sky
With a patch on my eye.
Like a pirate I'd be with wings,
Flying free.
The wings would be bold
And covered in gold.
I'd shoot into space
To start off a race,
For people who fly
With a patch on one eye.

Peter Stephens (9)
Raventhorpe Preparatory School

A Snowball Fight

We picked the teams,
We built a fort,
Sorted out tactics,
'Ready, aim, fire!'

Snowballs flying,
This way and that,
People being hit,
Our fort serving well.

'Time out, time out!'
They cried.
We started again.
Then *nooooo!*
Our fort fell down.

'Run and fire!'
I shout.
We did well
But we still lost.
'Better luck next time,'
They say.

We look back
At the melting battlefield,
Now more snow,
But just wait until next year!

Simon Warne (9)
Raventhorpe Preparatory School

Snow Day

I woke up one morning
So plainly to see
My favourite teddy
Right next to me

We opened the blind
And what did we find?
The land was all white
It gave us a fright

I helped Teddy to dress
And we went outside
We got out a sledge
To prepare for a ride

Well wrapped up against the snow
Over the fields
We started to go
It was great!

Nicole Burlinson (10)
Raventhorpe Preparatory School

Snow

Snow is a delicate powder,
It comes from the top of the sky,
It is pretty and twinkly,
Like diamonds, oh my!
Snow gives ice,
Snow gives pleasure,
To children it is quite a treasure,
It runs through your hands
And spreads a white carpet,
Across many lands,
Snow! Snow! Snow!

Charlotte Alderson (10)
Raventhorpe Preparatory School

Snow

Snow is very bright,
The colour of snow is white,
When it turns into ice,
It looks quite nice,
It looks like a blanket of white,
Glowing and shining at night,
In the streetlight,
Snow!

Saif Khalil (9)
Raventhorpe Preparatory School

My Snowy Rabbit

Once I had a rabbit
He was grey and white
We let him run around
He went across the ground
In the snow, full of glee
He was covered, whiter than white
We took him inside
To have his fur dried
My snowy rabbit.

Andrew Nicholson (9)
Raventhorpe Preparatory School

Snowman

S now falls silently
N ow it's here
O h it's cold
W here is it?
M elting snow
A good time
N ow it's gone.

Anthony Pardew (9)
Sunnybrow Primary School

The Sun

I can burn and blind anyone;
They will not have a very long life
Or a wife.
I can heat up
And beat up;
I am stronger than the wind
And I'm not very kind.
You wouldn't want to mess with me
Or you won't have a knee.
I'm more dangerous than a firework,
So don't mess with me, you jerk!

I can melt 100 freezers
And kill 200 geezers.
I can kill
And you will
Not want to see me in a mood
Or you will get chewed
Up and killed.
You will be milled
And not very chilled.
I can melt
And belt
A footy which is hard
And turn you into lard.
You will be barred, curled
Out of my world;
Your body will be curled.
Warning! Don't mess with me.

Chloe Thompson (10)
Sunnybrow Primary School

The Tornado

I can destroy houses
And kill the louses
I can spin around
And make you housebound

I will destroy all I see
And make you flee
I am mean and fiery
Spin, spin, spin

All my spinning makes me tired
So when I am restless
I go away, away, away.

Ross Stoker (10)
Sunnybrow Primary School

The Wind

I can strip leaves off the trees
I can throw the trees down
I am violent and angry and powerful
I can make the sea crash upon the rocks
I sometimes pile rubbish on your doorstep
I make you stay indoors all the time
When I get angry, I kill people
And when I'm cross
I sink ships to the bottom of the sea
What am I?
Wind.

Anthony Kirsopp (9)
Sunnybrow Primary School

I Can Swim Fast

I can swim fast, jump over waves in the sea
Show off my shiny skin to people
Who would like to see?
Swim, swim and swim
Flick my tail up in the air
Then dive into my secret lair

People catch me; take me to a cool pool
Just for money, people watch me
They think it's funny
Swim, swim and swim
To put me on show

They come on holiday to swim with me
They make me jump through hoops
They think that I'm not lonely but I am you see
So if you know who I am, come and see me
In the sea!

Laura Bartlett (10)
Sunnybrow Primary School

Joy

I am joy . . .
I roam like the sun making people warm inside
Pink, blue, green
I'm the brightest colours seen
I'm the biggest waterslide

I am joy . . .
I will make you feel like a football team
The winning side
People cheering your ride
Just watch the cup gleam.

Thomas Garrod (10)
Sunnybrow Primary School

Personification Poem

Why are you always happy?
Are you always happy?
Does it just hit you just like that?
Oh, if only you knew!
Do you just go out sad
Then at the click of your fingers you're happy?
Oh, I wish I knew
Instead of you.

Why are you always happy?
Were you born with happiness?

Did you get it from your parents,
Brothers, sisters
Or pets?

Oh, I wish I knew!

Chloe Woolf (10)
Sunnybrow Primary School

Hailstone

I could hurt you!
Really badly, very madly
And don't disturb me anymore
Or I'll come again, fiercely and gladly
To whip your body, face and hands
And anything else that it demands
To send you flinging away from me
Where you belong, inside you see
Then stand back and laugh at you, tee-hee!
A funny joke on you from me
The sun comes out
He's got the last laugh
For I return extremely fast
Now you will have a blast!

Craig Allinson (11)
Sunnybrow Primary School

The Hurricane

I am noisy, crazy, angry and strong
I can destroy towns and cities
And pick up cars and houses
I can give you frostbite with my freezing wind
I am happy when causing maximum destruction
I will pick up cars and throw them at you
So you will be as flat as a leaf that has been stood on
About fifty times!
You don't want to see me in a mood
I will curl you in a ball
And play football when you are in that ball
Beware! Watch out
If I am about!

Ryan Liddell (9)
Sunnybrow Primary School

Personification Poem

I can make the hairs stick up
On the back of your neck

As straight as a telegraph pole
I am sneaky and mean

I'll crawl all over you
And when you're asleep
I'll stick my claws into you
So silent and deep
That you will never
Be alive again.

Connor Coulson (11)
Sunnybrow Primary School

Snowstorm

S nowflakes falling like leaves,
N ow it's cold outside,
O w! Snowballs in your face,
W arm inside,
S ledging, people sledging down hills,
T owering snow shelters with people inside,
O uch! Snowballs in your chest,
R olling huge snowballs,
M ad snowball fights.

Luke Newton (9)
Sunnybrow Primary School

Snowstorm

S nowmen are being built
N obody knows
O w! Snowballs get thrown
W hat a wonderful time
S nowflakes falling silently
T otal snow madness
O h people love building snowmen
R ings of snow fill the ground
M any children play all day.

Shannen Wilson (9)
Sunnybrow Primary School

The Snowman

S nowmen dance around in the snow,
N ow the time has come
O h, it's such an exciting day
W ow, aren't you going to come?
M ums and dads tell you off
A nd snowmen are being built
N ow it's all gone away.

Rachael Thompson (9)
Sunnybrow Primary School

Class Three

C lass Three is the funniest class
L oads of children
A ngry teachers shout all day
S isters and brothers may be there
S ometimes good, sometimes bad

T eachers help us to learn
H ere we come and here we go
R espect we need
E verybody enjoys themselves
E xcited children.

James Matthews (8)
Sunnybrow Primary School

Snowman

S nowmen melt when the sun comes out,
N obody gets anywhere when the roads are icy,
O ut we go to have lots of fun,
W ind gets too strong for us to play,
M en and women help their children build snowmen,
A nd now it's time for us to go in,
N ow the snow is going away.

Chelsea Stoker (9)
Sunnybrow Primary School

Dad's Bike

My dad has a motorbike
That's as fast as the speed of light
He rides it nearly all the time
I can't wait until
I take flight on my dad's motorbike.

Rory Adey (9)
The Chorister School

Horse

Back feet kicker
Human licker

Obstacle jumper
Very fast runner

Hunter lover
Cowboy stunner.

Jacob Bushnell (7)
The Chorister School

Tortoise

Slow walker
Bad talker
Leaf eater
Hunted creature
Shell hider
Good disguiser.

Aidan Jagger (9)
The Chorister School

Lion

Pretty elegant
Pretty intelligent
Roaring beast
Eating meat.

Charlotte Tait (8)
The Chorister School

Walking Alone In The Dark

Dark trees are like
Man-eating monsters watching me
The whistling wind is like
A shrill warning me to go back
Owls hooting are like screams
From people in danger
Stars are like little eyes
Watching my every move
Bushes are like lions
Ready to pounce
Crickets chirping are like spies
Ready to shoot!
So altogether
Walking alone in the dark
Is not my favourite thing!

Piers Broadfoot (11)
The Chorister School

Boo!

Sitting in a tree one day
Thinking what to do
I thought I could
J
U
M
Down P and
Scare my friend with a
Boo!

Alice Brown (9)
The Chorister School

The Lord Of The Rings: The Dark Walk

In a forest with dark trees
Like Ents watching me,
The full moon
Like Sauron's Eye
Watching me.

The bushes rustling
Like Gollum chasing me,
The owls hooting
Like Nazgul speaking.

The red leaves in autumn
Like the blood that was spilt,
From the Middle-Earth war
Sticks getting snapped and crunched,
Like Orcs after me or
Orcs making camp.

When I hear a little waterfall
I think it's the home of the elves,
(Rivendell),
When branches fall
I think it's Orcs shooting me.

Oisín Keating (9)
The Chorister School

Spider

Sky rider
Fly binder
Web spinner
Fly dinner.

Elliot Macdonald (9)
The Chorister School

The Forest

I am scared in a really dark wood
With the full moon
Like a face watching me
It is also when the werewolves come out
The 'normal' wolves are howling
Like people shouting 'Help!'
I can hear the air whizzing round me
Like zombies' cries
Gates are slamming
Like guns being shot
And thunder and lightning crashing down on the Earth
I feel like there is a ghost behind me
I turn around
I wake up
It was just a dream
I lay down on my bed
Wondering.

Samuel Storer (10)
The Chorister School

Koala

Great sleeper
Super dreamer

Moves slowly
Eats lonely

Smooth skin
Not thin

Hard butt
Small foot

Big claws
Tiny jaws.

Elliot Lydon (9)
The Chorister School

Changes

I look out of the window
And fall into a dream
Multicoloured umbrellas
Change into colourful candy
The lashes of rain
Change into rays of sunshine
Wellington boots
Change into sandals with open toes
Waterproof jackets
Change into beach towels
Pools of muddy water
Change to moats of sandcastles
Children paddling in warm seas
Rather than cold puddles
Miserable grey November faces
Change to bright tanned smiling faces of summer
Drumming of raindrops on rooftops in the city
Change to the beating down of the sun onto villas in Spain
November to August
In a second
Oh, I wish!

Alice Doherty (11)
The Chorister School

Pig

Big eater
Deep breather

Sunbather
Noisy sleeper

Big breeder
Snorty creature

Mud hutter
Loves the gutter.

Holly Lindley (9)
The Chorister School

Walking Alone In The Dark!

I'm playing in the park
It turns dark
I'm alone
The dark trees look like blackbirds
Watching me
The owls sound like ghostly cries
The moon's watching me
The branches look like hands
Trying to grab me
People look like ghosts
Help me - I'm all alone!

The tree roots look like snakes
The trunk looks like a giant
Trying to eat me
The falling leaves look like bats
People look like ghosts
Help me - I'm all alone!

Georgia Forbes (10)
The Chorister School

Hippo

Fat squasher
Big washer

Good eater
Fine beater

Wide waddler
Giant toddler

Slow swimmer
Lakes quiver.

Alex Goulding (8)
The Chorister School

The Midnight Roar Of Traffic

When I hear a motorbike
I think a lion's right behind me roaring ferociously.
When I see lamp posts at night
Yellow eyes are watching me!
I hate it in the night when few cars are going past
And all of the street is dead quiet.
Then it starts to rain,
Like balls of hail
Trying to steer me to my doom.
Suddenly a train speeds
Across a bridge nearby
Like a car trying to
Whip me up and blow me away.
Then it does and I fall into a river,
A ship sails along, moves on top of me,
So I go down to 'Davy Jones' locker.

John-Paul Moberly (9)
The Chorister School

Walking Alone In The Dark

I was walking home one night
I tried to take a shortcut
But I'm lost in the
Woods by myself
But other people are here too
Tall dark trees
Looking like foot tall people
People are muttering
But it's only the leaves rustling
The moon is looking down at me
Like a smiley face
The wind is like a whisper far, far away
An owl's hoot sounds like a ghost cry
The city lights far away
Gleaming at me . . . like cat's eyes.

John Anderson (10)
The Chorister School

Walking Alone In The Dark Wood

I hate the dark, rustling bushes,
Like a werewolf lying in wait.
The trees are very dark and tall,
Like witches about to grab me!
I hear owls hooting in the dark,
Like faint ghostly cries!
I see yellow menacing eyes in the trees,
Like an evil monster lurking in the shadows.
A dog barking far way,
Sounds like a big bear roaring.
A tree stump in the dark
Looks like a giant spider out to get me!
I am running along the path
Seeing the stars sparkling in the sky
Then I am filled with joy
As I come to the safety and warmth of my home.

Thomas Lydon (10)
The Chorister School

Walking Alone

Walking alone in the dark
Feels like someone's following me
Dark trees are like fingers reaching out for me
Leaves rustling on the ground,
Footsteps coming for me.
I look up, a full moon -
It feels like someone's always watching me.
Owls hooting sound like ghostly cries!
Insects moving along and under the ground
Sound like people ready for the kill
Bats in trees, eyes glowing so bright
Look like wolves about to pounce and kill -
Walking alone feels ever so cold!

Henry Pemberton (11)
The Chorister School

Walking Through The Dark Forest

I am walking through the wood at night
It seems very creepy
I hear the rustling of the leaves
Like an animal stalking me
Small stars gleaming in the sky
Like small bits of hope emerging as I walk
Crows flying over my head
Like small dragons fighting above
Huge looming trees
Like towering monsters
A woodpecker tapping
Like a prisoner shaking his bars
Flocks of crowing birds
Like a slave crying out
All of these scary thoughts stayed worryingly in my head
Until I came out of the dark wood.

James Matthews (10)
The Chorister School

The Forest At Night

The forest at night is really creepy
I hate the sound of insects
It feels as if my eardrums are busting
I hate the full moon
It is as if there was a spy watching my every move
As I move the owls light up my path
With their eyes
I hate the shadows behind me
They are like sneaky, creepy ghosts
But what I really hate are
The twigs snapping like pistol shots
It is like someone jumping on your back
When you don't expect it
The forest is spooky at night!

William Dooley (10)
The Chorister School

The Creepy Night

It was a dark creepy night
There was a distant flickering light
It reminded me of a wizard's sparkly eye
I heard a noise
It sounded like a huntsman coming to get me
I turned around and began to scream
There was a figure, dark as can be
It reminded me of a zombie sneaking towards me
I turned back round and toddled along
I began to see swaying vines blowing around
It reminded me of a witch's tatty hair
I began to feel drowsy
Bang!
It was gone
What a relief
It was just a dream.

Freddie Wintrip (11)
The Chorister School

Alone In The Darkness

I hate the full moon
It's like a big eye
Watching you

I hate the barbed wire fences
Like a lion tamer's whip
Trying to slash you

I hate the babbling water
Like ghosts whispering

I hate the owls hooting
As if a lost soul
Is trying to get
Revenge.

Adam Waugh (9)
The Chorister School

In My Cage

In my cage I feel like I'm in a prison cell,
Once I tried to escape,
I got caught and thrown back in.

The carrots are just as bad,
They look like giant orange slugs,
Urgh!

I feel life is just unfair!

I'm thirsty,
The water looks refreshing and cool,
Until it enters my mouth,
It tastes like blood,
I spit the rest out.

I'm really ravenous!
I walk over to my salt lick
A car wheel is coming to kill me!

I go to have some food,
It wriggles into my mouth,
It feels like maggots
Running down my throat,
I feel sick.

I go down to enter my bed,
When I walk over the wood shavings
I hear animal claws wanting to scratch me,
I get to my bed,

A nice long rest will do.

Lyndsay Connor (9)
The Chorister School

Walking Alone In The Dark!

Walking through a wood
Makes me feel scared

When owls hoot
I think people are whispering things about me

Dark trees with shadows
Are like monsters hanging over me

When I walk through the black grass
I feel like I'm walking through the sea

When I see the moon
It's like a big face

And then I see the stars
They're like twinkling eyes
They make me feel safe.

Sophie Phillips (11)
The Chorister School

A Dark Walk Home

I was walking home in the dark
A woodpecker scraping the wood
It sounds like an entrapped prisoner
I started walking quicker
The wind blows and the bushes bend
Like monsters beckoning me to come
I take no notice

An owl hoots like a ghost's cry
I speed up and see my house
But it's just a man with a lantern
Giant dark trees bend over me
Like monsters frozen in time
Then a light symbolises my house
I run as fast as I can, home!

Dominic Cockburn (10)
The Chorister School

In The Dark

I'm in the woods,
All on my own . . . or am I?
The trees around,
Swaying menacingly,
They look like monsters,
Arms out wide.
I look up
To see a giant face,
No, wait!
It is the moon.
Lights from distant towns,
Stare at me like eyes.
Bats high in the trees,
Like monsters hidden away.
Owls up high in the trees,
Hooting like crying birds,
I hear crunching leaves,
Is that whispering behind me?
Shadows on the ground,
Look!
Someone's chasing after me,
I run, I run back home,
When I get back,
I find out,
That they were just shadows of trees!

James Roberts (10)
The Chorister School